Red Bugs, Moonshine and The Book of Leviticus

Emerald
Coast
Publishing

Destin, Florida

Red Bugs, Moonshine and The Book of Leviticus

Election 2000—Florida Hasn't Seen A Fight this Good Since Orlando Hosted the Southern Baptist Convention

Ken Revell

Emerald Coast Publishing

Destin, Florida

RED BUGS, MOONSHINE AND THE BOOK OF LEVITICUS:
ELECTION 2000—FLORIDA HASN'T SEEN A FIGHT THIS GOOD
SINCE ORLANDO HOSTED THE SOUTHERN BAPTIST CONVENTION

Emerald Coast Publishing
P.O Box 1879
Destin, FL 32541

The author wishes to acknowledge the contribution of Eric and Meg in
the morning @ Sunny 98.5 for the concept and much of the text of
"Palm Beach Pokey." They are printed here with permission. Wally
Gator, Mr. Twiddle, Magilla Gorilla and the Wally Gator theme song
are registered trademarks and copyright © Hanna-Barbera Productions,
Inc. Bullwinkle, Rocky J. Squirrel and Dudley Do-Right are registered
trademarks and copyright ©, Jay Ward Productions, Inc. The use of the
same falls under the fair use provisions of 17 U.S.C. § 107.

All Scripture quotations are from the HOLY BIBLE, NEW
INTERNATIONAL VERSION®, Copyright © 1973, 1978, 1984 by
International Bible Society. Used by permission of Zondervan
Publishing House. All rights reserved. The "NIV" and "New
International Version" trademarks are registered in the United States
Patent and Trademark Office by International Bible Society. Use of
either trademark requires the permission of International Bible Society.

Library of Congress Cataloging-in-Publication Data applied for.

ISBN 0-9707949-0-8

FIRST EDITION

This book is dedicated to:

My Grandmother, Alwayne Rumph Cook—the original "Steel Magnolia" and

My Uncle, Jerry L. Bennett, United States Naval Academy, Class of '61, who dragged me, as a child, from Jamestown to Williamsburg to Shiloh to Andersonville and all points in between, and taught me to SEE the miracle of America.

Acknowledgements

I would like to thank the following people who helped me greatly in writing this book. My wife, Tasha, and my mother-in-law, Maxine. I would also like to thank my son, Joshua Caleb "Governor Boudreaux," who regularly awakened me at 3:00 a.m. to care for him and write another column, usually with him in one arm.

Finally, I would like to thank Albert Gore, Jr., Bill Daley and Gore attorney, David Boies, without whose assistance this book would not have been possible. (I couldn't have made this stuff up in a million years).

Contents

IV

MUSTER THE TROOPS,
THERE'S GENOCIDE IN BOSNIA

V

HILLARY, QUEEN OF DENILE

VI

RUMINATIONS OF A PHOBAPHOBIC ZOOPHILE

VII

THE BIG EVENT . . . GOES INTO OVERTIME

VIII

OK. IT'S DOUBLE OVERTIME

IX

HAVE WE BEEN CHAD?

X

THE FINAL COUNT—NO REALLY,
I MEAN IT THIS TIME

XI

BILL DALEY—WON'T YOU PLEASE GO HOME

XII

WHAT'S NEXT? HOW WOULD I KNOW . . . DO I LOOK LIKE JEANE DIXON?

XIII

EPILOGUE

At a time like this, scorching irony, not convincing argument, is needed. O! Had I the ability, and could reach the nation's ear, I would today, pour out a fiery stream of biting ridicule, blasting reproach, withering sarcasm, and stern rebuke. For it is not light that is needed, but fire; it is not the gentle shower, but thunder. We need the storm, the whirlwind, the earthquake. The feeling of the nation must be quickened; the conscience of the nation must be roused; the propriety of the nation must be startled; the hypocrisy of the nation must be exposed; its crimes against God and man must be proclaimed and denounced.

--Frederick Douglass

Introduction

The 2000 Presidential election is finally in the books. Finally. Whatever else you may say about former V.P. Albert and his merry men, they sure know how to stir up a stink right out of thin air, don't they?

On November 7, we had an election here in the Sunshine State. Bush won by 1,784 votes. A squeaker. We had a re-count. Bush won again.

Albert & Co. sent their main-most crook, Bill Daley, down here to squawk about the ballot in Palm Beach County and to "dig up" a few more votes. They wanted a hand re-re-count in three heavily Democratic counties, in which the county canvassing boards were all controlled by Democrats. Florida Secretary of State, Harris, told the canvassing boards, "You can count 'till the cows come home, but you need to know; Florida law says the cows come home November 14th, at 5:00 p.m."

The Demos, fearing that they might not dig up enough votes before Elsie came in from the field, sued Secretary Harris. The presiding judge, Terry Lewis, another Democrat, ruled that the Secretary can make the call. That's the law.

The Demos didn't like that either, so they whined on to the Florida Supreme Court—all Democrats and oooohhhhh, just a little bit partisan. The Florida Supremes ordered Secretary Harris not to certify the states' vote, and then changed the law to give Albert more time to come up with the votes to win.

Albert & Co. still couldn't dig up the votes by the deadline, so Secretary Harris "certified" Florida's vote for

Bush. Meanwhile the Sho' 'Nuff Supremes stepped in to consider whether the Florida Supremes had acted illegally, and Albert went on and sued the counties directly.

The case against the counties was tried by Judge Sauls—a native *North Florida* Democrat (not to be confused with the South Florida species of the same name). Albert's lawyers put on two witnesses to *prove* their case. One was a political science major who tried to find excuses why a "chad" might not fall out of a punch card. "Maybe they put it on top of the metal box and pressed on it," he speculated. "Or maybe chads built up from previous votes and prevented the 'chad' from falling out," or "maybe the rubber in the voting device had hardened and the 'chad' just wouldn't push through." The Bush lawyers objected, saying, "this man is no rubber expert!" (Where's Dr. Ruth when you need her?) The Gore team next called a statistician who finally admitted, when cross examined by the Bush people, that he really didn't have a clue as to whether there were enough dimpled ballots to change the outcome of the election.

Meanwhile, the Sho' 'Nuff Supremes fired a shot across the bow of the Florida Supremes, canceling their previous order, and basically saying "This ain't an election for Leon County Dog Catcher (that would be completely 'yo' bidness'), but the U.S. Constitution and federal law does have a little something to say about the election of the President. You need to keep that in mind."

A couple of hours later, back in Tallahassee, Judge Sauls ruled that Albert had failed to prove his case. Gore lawyers ran back to the Florida Supremes, who ignored the warning of the Sho' 'Nuff Supremes and re-extended their own deadline. This time, three of the Florida Justices (including Chief Little Chuckie himself) couldn't stomach the decision, and abandoned the sinking liberal ship. The majority, however, ordered re-re-re-counts of *certain* votes in 64 of Florida's 67 counties.

At this point Seven of the nine justices on the U.S. Supreme Court agreed that there were significant Constitutional problems in the way in which the Florida Supreme Court was conducting this orchestra. The question was, "what to do about it?" The majority just said, "stop the show and give us that baton."

I was just thinking. How did Florida ever get into this mess? We haven't seen a fight this good since Orlando hosted the Southern Baptist Convention. How did we get here?

First, your compass won't work here in Florida where the further south you go, the further north you get. North Florida is southern and conservative, while the South I-95 corridor (Dade, Broward and Palm Beach counties) are for the most part northern and liberal.

The following compilation of columns logs the course of this fiasco, from a North Florida (southern) perspective. This book will also give you insight into North Florida sometimes through the eyes of a child. It will help those of you "who ain't from around here" get a glimpse of why we are the way we are. If you think a child raised in Wakulla County thinks anything like a child raised in the streets of Miami; think again. How did we get here? Read on, and let me explain this one.

II

Geriatric Debating

Geriatric Debating

In Florida, we have more old folks per acre than any other place on earth . . . and they all vote—well, at least they try to.

Geriatric Debating? . . . No, it's not a new Olympic event, at least not yet. Maybe it should be. If you witnessed last night's presidential debate, I think you would agree that we've got the gold medal locked down on that one. You would think that they were running for President of the South I-95 corridor.

Gore says he's going to get prescription drugs for the elderly through Medicare. Bush says he too wants seniors to have prescription drugs, but that Gore has had eight years to get 'em the drugs. (this whole debate is sounding more and more like a back-alley street deal in the Bronx). "You've had your chance, Vice President. You're just running on Mediscare, trying to frighten people into the voting booth." And, to prove that he cares even more about the elderly than Gore, Bush proposes "Vision Care" be added to Medicare.

Gore says he will put Medicare and Social Security in an iron-clad lock box. He'll only peek inside occasionally to make sure that the Republicans haven't run off with it.

GORE: Let me just give you one quick example. There's an elderly moose in the audience here tonight named Bullwinkle, he's from Milwaukee. He's seventy years old, he has high blood pressure and his alternative lifestyle live in lover, Rocky J. Squirrel has heart trouble. Governor Bush and his kind have denied this lovely couple

23

the right to marry and adopt children. They are therefore all alone in this, their golden years. The sole source of their meager income is from television royalties and is less than $25,000 a year. They can't afford their prescription drugs, so they have to go to Canada where a former law enforcement officer and friend, Dudley Do-right, is able to slip them a few pills. I find this appalling. It's just one more example of the heartless Republican policy.

BUSH: What the hell does Bullwinkle and Rocky have to do with this?

GORE: See, I told you he was heartless.

BUSH: Its fuzzy math he uses. Trying to scare people and mooses and squirrels too, I suppose, into the voting booth. I'm beginning to think that he not only invented the internet, but he invented the calculator too.

LEHRER: Let me ask you both this, and we'll move on, on this subject. As a practical matter, both of you want to bring prescription drugs to seniors, correct?

BUSH: Correct.

GORE: Correct, but the difference is − the difference is I want to bring it to 100 percent, and he brings it only to 5 percent.

LEHRER: All right. All right. All right.

BUSH: That's just -- that's just -- that's just totally false.

LEHRER: All right. What difference does it make how...

BUSH: Wait a minute. It's just totally false for him to stand up here and say that. Let me make sure the seniors hear me loud and clear. They've had their chance to get something done. I'm going to work with both Republicans and Democrats to reform the system. All seniors will be covered. All poor seniors will have their prescription drugs paid for. In the meantime -- in the meantime, we're going to have a plan to help poor seniors. And "in the meantime" could be one year or two years.

GORE: Let me -- let me call your attention to the key word there. He said all "poor" seniors.

BUSH: No. Wait a minute, all seniors are covered under prescription drugs in my plan.

GORE: In the first year? In the first year?

BUSH: If we can get it done in the first year, you bet. Yours is phased in in eight years.

GORE: No. No. No. No. It's a two-phase plan, Jim. And for the first four years -- it takes a year to pass it. And for the first four years, only the poor are covered. Middle class seniors, like Bullwinkle and Rocky J. Squirrel are not covered for four to five years.

LEHRER: I've got an idea.

GORE: OK.

LEHRER: You have any more to say about this, you can say it in your closing statement, so we'll move on, OK?

New question, Vice President Gore, how would you contrast your approach to preventing future -- future oil price and supply problems like we have now to the approach of Governor Bush?

GORE: Excellent question, and here's the—here's the simple difference: My plan would provide all the free oil that seniors could ever use or hope to use.

BUSH: What the hell do seniors have to do with OPEC and our reliance on middle eastern oil?

GORE: Mean, mean, mean. I told you he was mean.

LEHRER: All right, Governor, on the Supreme Court question, should a voter assume—you're pro-life?

BUSH: I am pro-life.

GORE: I am pro-abortion, but I want all the seniors out there to know that I am awfully glad that we didn't have abortions back when they were born, because a lot of them wouldn't be here today.

BUSH: Your Social Security lock box would be a lot smaller wouldn't it, Al?

LEHRER: What kind of President would each of you make?

BUSH: I would make a good President. He would make a bad one.

LEHRER: No. No. I meant only for each of you to comment on yourself, not your opponent.

BUSH: Oh, sorry Jim.

GORE: If I'm entrusted with the Presidency, here are the choices that I will make: I'll balance the budget. I'll pay off the national debt. I'll put Medicare and Social Security in a lockbox and protect it. I'll hide the box under my bed. I will cut taxes and I will provide a welfare program for anyone who thinks he needs it.

BUSH: Could I follow up here, Jim?

LEHRER: Go ahead Governor.

BUSH: I just want to say that a herd of Texas Longhorns couldn't produce that much bull in a month of Sundays.

Jeb and the He Coon

Although the Presidential candidates have raised Geriatric Debating to unprecedented new heights; W. witnessed his little brother Jeb take a butt-whipping from the elderly in his first shot at the Florida Governor's office, and W. wasn't about to be out "old folked" by Gore now. You recall that debate between Governor Chiles and Jeb—don't you?

November 2, 1994

The Florida governor's race ended last night. No, the election is not until next week, but it's over just the same. That's a shame. Republican candidate Jeb Bush and incumbent Governor Lawton Chiles had this, their third and final debate. It was aired statewide. According to the polls, Jeb was ahead going into the debate. The morning paper says nothing about the philosophical differences between the candidates. It says nothing about taxes, abortion, prisons, education, or school vouchers. Why? Because the lesser experienced Bush committed political suicide, and the Governor played taps for the funeral.

Chiles, an "ol' country lawyer," is apparently familiar with the legal cliché; "If the law is on your side, talk about the law. If the facts are on your side, talk about the facts. If neither one is on your side, talk about something else," and that's what he did.

Jeb Bush is a young man. Chiles is an old man. Florida is packed with old people . . . and they all vote. When Jeb referred to the Governor as an "OLD" liberal, the Governor shook his finger in Jeb's face, right there on TV while the whole state watched. It may as well have been the finger of two or three million old people throughout the state.

Then Jeb unwittingly played "straight man," setting Chiles up for another of his famous "crackerisms." Jeb said something in Spanish and then offered Chiles the translation.

"What I've just said Governor," Bush explained, "is the governor needs to lead and the government needs to know how to sell." Jeb was sounding like a smart-aleck. I saw it coming and said it aloud, "Don't go there Jeb!" The Governor then responded, "I know how to lead and I know how to sell, and if I can reply to you in 'cracker'; The ol' he-coon walks just before the light of day."

"Well that's it, it's over," I said, and then, realizing that crying wouldn't do any good—I began to laugh. I thought about some of Chiles' other crackerisms, like; "It's a sorry frog, who won't holler in his own pond," or; "Even a blind hog will root out an acorn, once in a while." I laughed harder.

My wife looked at me as if I had lost my mind. "What's so funny?" she asked, "and what does that he-coon thing mean?"

"It means the Governor just got re-elected and he knows it," I responded.

"Have I missed something here?" my wife asked.

"Honey, it means this: I am very happy that you speak Spanish so well. Your mother must be very proud of you, but this ain't Tijuana, this is Florida. You ain't from around here, are you? Oh, where are my manners? I almost forgot to thank you for handing me the election."

At that point, my wife just got up and walked down the hall muttering something about "you people."

29

P.S. Try again next time Jeb, we need your ideas, but remember; be humble, 'cause nobody likes a smart-aleck.

Jeb Ain't Stupid No More

November 3, 1998

Once again, it's election day here in the Sunshine State. Yee-Haw! Lt. Governor Buddy McKay is doing his best to hold on to the mansion for the Democrats, but there are problems with him doing so. McKay is a nice man, but he ain't the "He Coon." Yes, the Governor has stumped all over the state pushing McKay, but every time Chiles opens his mouth, it reminds the crowd that he is not a candidate in this race. Too bad for the Democrats. He would have been the Demos only hope. The Governor is a communicator. I say better than Reagan. He uses the stump as an opportunity to speak directly to the people rather than to the press. He is homespun and colorful. He is educated, but doesn't allow it to get in his way.

Florida is becoming an increasingly Republican state. The Clinton/Gore Administration is largely responsible for that occurring. Clinton's complete dereliction of his duties to the military, and the administration's ongoing attempt to turn the Department of Defense into UNPD Blues, has riled more than a few. The Panhandle, with Tyndall AFB, the Naval Coastal Systems Station, Eglin AFB, NAS Pensacola, Hurlbert Field, Duke Field and Whiting Field will not be carried by a Democrat today even if hell does freeze over. Joe Scarborough could run "nekkid" down Highway 98 all the way from Pensacola to Panama City and still get 70 percent of the vote in our district. Won't the Demos ever understand that a prepared military deters aggression. And another thing—why should someone retire from Microsoft or General Electric and have

31

it better than those who have spent their lives protecting our nation. That just don't make no sense to me.

"Clinton/Gore" have done to Florida what they have done to the nation—driven a wedge of division between us. Sure the Demos still have support along the I-95 corridor from Palm Beach County to Miami, but if the Congress actually found a popular cure to the Social Security dilemma, that support would vanish faster than Jimmy Hoffa.

Maybe it's not all that bad—the division. No one can get elected in a state-wide tally here anymore, unless they are able to draw some votes across party lines. In the future we will see statewide elections handled in one of two ways. The party candidates will either be more civil and more to the center or they will set in their positions like concrete and "lie" like a dog about their opponents. The Democrats will be the Party of fiscal irresponsibility who only get elected with promises of bigger government "relief" checks and by scaring the hell out of great aunt Carolyn with tales of the big bad Republican wolf that eats Social Security checks. The Republicans will of course be portrayed as the party of the rich and the haters of the poor. Which approach will they choose? Yeah, I know, but wasn't it nice to think about it for a moment?

The last time that Jeb ran, he blew the election and he has learned from it. The "He Coon" said afterward, "They just tried to put him in a grade he wasn't ready for yet." Jeb's former "cockiness" is gone. He now seems as willing to learn as to teach. Jeb ain't stupid no more.

When the votes are counted, Jeb Bush will indeed be the newly elected governor of Florida. I haven't always called them right, but you can take this one to the bank.

The "Ol' He-Coon" Has Up and Died

Tallahassee, December 12, 1998.

"Cracker" Governor Lawton Mainor Chiles died today. He was last seen walking his dog Tess. Tess was a starving old mutt that started hanging around the gate at the Governor's Mansion. Chiles invited her in to become Florida's "First Dog." Tess and the Governor were alone in the exercise room of the cabana behind the mansion when he died from a heart fibrillation twenty three days before his voluntary retirement from public life.

If it does indeed, "take one to know one," I can report for certainty that the Governor was the quintessential Florida "cracker." Crackers are an endangered species in this state. It was Chiles who once noted, "Florida is the only state in this country where the further south you go—the further north you get." He was who he was and he had no need for a Hollywood image maker to turn him into something he was not. There is no doubt that he was an occasional embarrassment to the pompous sophisticates of Miami, but he was, to many Floridians, the salt of Florida's political earth. First elected to the Florida House in 1959, Chiles later served in the State Senate and was elected in 1970 to the U.S. Senate. In that campaign, Chiles walked from the tiny town of Century in Northwest Florida, all the way to Miami, a distance of more than 1,000 miles

He ate and slept in the homes of ordinary citizens along the way. He listened to their concerns. "Walkin' Lawton," they called him. After eighteen years of fighting gridlock in the U.S. Senate, he just up and quit. "I feel like

33

I can't get anything accomplished here," Chiles explained. He once said, "I didn't come here to stay, I came here to make a difference." Buddy McKay and Connie Mack slugged it out fighting to get Chile's senate seat. In the closest election in Florida history, Mack won. McKay went to Chiles and begged him to come out of retirement and run for governor. McKay would fill in the number two slot on the ticket. Chiles agreed. They won.

Chiles was often labeled by press and foe alike, as a "populist." He was not. He was the product of a time and place where people genuinely cared for their neighbors. Those who are not such a product find labels to explain away the actions of those who are.

When tornadoes ripped through the state last winter, the Governor lead a host of politicians, emergency workers and press through the hinterlands where the destruction had occurred. When the caravan came upon a woman standing in front of a small frame house that had been blown to smithereens, the Governor ordered his driver to stop. Everyone got out of the vehicles. The Governor ran down to the edge of a mud filled gully that separated him and the hysterically crying woman. He jumped the ditch, oblivious to the mud, which now covered his boots and the lower legs of his pants. The old Governor ran to the crying woman as everyone else stood at the pavement. He put his arms around her and she leaned into him for support. The Governor did all he could do at that moment. He cared.

One of the politicians standing on the road commented "He is a masterful populist." A columnist that I know well, standing next to him jotted in his notebook, "Chiles service to his people has spanned five decades. He has never lost an election. It is because he cares. Whether you agree with his policies or not, he does genuinely care.

I hope that the ass standing next to me gets defeated in his next election, because he doesn't care. I guess he doesn't want to get mud on his Guccis."

Good-bye Governor.

The Repubs Want the Breaux Pres.

Naw, you idiot, not John Breaux, Jeb's breaux.
It seems that Governor Bush's older brother George W., who happens to be the Governor of Texas, is now after the same job that their daddy got fired from in 1992. It was a religious firing. It was our golden calf—"the economy stupid," and the Democrats asked us to bow down as a nation and worship it. We did. The Demos danced in the streets. It was the beginning of the greatest moral decline in the history of our nation. The Clinton-Gore Administration has succeeded in dividing us like we have never been divided since the war for Southern Independence.

They have convinced us that, whether we be black or white or Hispanic or Asian or Cuban that we have only personal or group desires and that the other groups are hell bent on keeping ours unfulfilled. They have pitted us, young, old or somewhere in between, each against the other. "Junior doesn't want to pay for Social Security anymore, Gramps," and "the eeeevile Republicans are going to help him cut you off." Male against female. Married against singles. Married with children vs. those without either. Single with children vs. everybody else. Jew against Gentile. Catholic against Protestant. Poor against middle class and both of them against the rich. You had better be suspicious and trust no one outside of your group because everybody else is out to get you.

If Lyndon Johnson delivered a state of the Union speech today beginning in his usual manner, "My fellow 'mericans," most of the country would turn the channel to

Jerry Springer. Wong Chu Lee, Tyrone Jefferson, Saul Rosenberg, Abdul Haddad, Dexter Thornbush and Gloria Mankiller would all think that Johnson was only addressing elderly gray Protestant Texas males with big ears.

They want you to believe that everyone is out to get you. That is everyone but Clinton-Gore—they "feel your pain." Hogwash. They crave your vote. JFK couldn't get elected in this environment. He'd say, "Ask not what your country can do for you, but what you can do for your country," and every group that looks to the government as the source of their strength and wealth; as their god, would throw up on his shoes.

We have more "phobes" than you can shake a stick at. Ok, at which you can shake a stick. (Happy now, you "grammar-phobe?") We have the speech police telling us what we can and can't say. The thought police telling us what we can and can't think. We have hate crimes. If someone named Einstein kills someone named Rosenblatt—that's a murder. If someone named Washington kills Rosenblatt—watch out—it may be a hate crime. Hate crime—smate crime, it's obvious either way, somebody had it in for Rosenblatt.

When one human being intentionally takes the life of another human being, that is horrific. Human life is still valuable in this country, isn't it? Oh no! I guess I've offended the pro-abortion people again, and you know how I detest offending anyone. Men shouldn't be able to comment on things such as abortion—only women have babies. Isn't that the same argument espoused by the lunatic that Clinton nominated to head the Civil Rights Division of the Justice Department. I can't remember her name. I'm glad. She wrote that black people shouldn't be required to adhere to laws that were enacted by a white

37

society. Where did he find her—the Arkansas Home for the Criminally insane?

Why did you get me off on all of this stuff? Oh, that's another thing, Clinton-Gore has brought us: if you screw up, it's always somebody else's fault.

What was this column about anyway? Oh Yeah. Florida Republicans want George W. elected in the worst way. So much, in fact, that many have traveled to New Hampshire risking life and limb in that frozen tundra, to help him secure the nomination. Not me. I wouldn't go up there if Mike Tyson threatened to bite off both of my ears.

I suppose the Florida Repubs and Jeb's breaux share common philosophies on the role of government in our lives. Come to think of it, I guess that when the next Hurricane Andrew or Opal slams us, it wouldn't hurt to have the Gov's breaux be the tallest hog at the trough. Go Breaux.

Liar, Liar Pants on Fire

Finally the primaries are over. Thank God. I think that I am about to write the only thing that I have ever written, that all of America would agree with. Ok, ok. With which all of America would agree. <u>This whole election process is entirely too long</u>. There, I wrote it. I am already sick of it and we still have the better part of a year in which our collective intelligence will be assaulted by more sorties of lies than all of the skud missiles that Daddy Bush dropped on Iraq. If you don't believe that, then punch; (a) ignorant or (b) stupid. I hope you punched "(a)" because "(b)" is often a permanent condition.

I see this one coming. Gore will carry liberal New York and most of the northeast, Illinois and Michigan, which are currently being held hostage by union extremists, and of course the left coast. And lest any of us forget, right here in our own beloved "Land of Flowers," Florida, the lower I-95 corridor. Why Dade, Broward and Palm Beach Counties? The same old tried and true—"they want to take away your Social Security check." How the same fish bites the same hook time after time after time amazes me. We send billions of dollars around the world to educate the uneducated, while ignorance thrives here among us. Amazing. Absolutely amazing.

Why Michigan? AFLCIO. And that ain't the Alachua Florida Citizens Improvement Organization, either. Why Illinois? Gore has the full backing of Richard J. Daley. I know, he's dead, but that's never stopped people from voting in Illinois before, has it? California? If you need an explanation for that one, then you punched "(b)" or you may have even punched both. If so, we count

39

that as a "(b)." Distortions, half truths and bald faced lies; Al Gore, ain't he a hoot. Well, he did invent the internet, you know. Yeah, and my uncle Jean-Thomas' goat, Pierre, is a PH damn D.

III

Say It Ain't So Joe . . .
Say It Ain't So

Gore Picks ... Lieberman ...
Joe Lieberman?

Al Gore has selected Connecticut Senator Joe Lieberman as his running mate for the upcoming presidential race. I don't find it odd that Gore would select a good man like Lieberman. Gore will do anything to win. If there is one thing the Democratic ticket needs in this race—it is an honest candidate. I do however find it odd that Lieberman has accepted. Joe, you are a decent man, and you do not need their stink on you. It will tarnish you forever.

We all remember Joe's speech on the floor of the U.S. Senate when the proverbial smoking gun, or "smoking dress" as the case may be, told on the President. Here's the pertinent part of it:

"Mr. President, I rise today to make a most difficult and distasteful statement. For me, probably the most difficult statement I've made on this floor in the 10 years I've been a member of the United States Senate.

On August 17th, President Clinton testified before a grand jury convened by the independent counsel, and then talked to the American people about his relationship with Monica Lewinsky, a former White House intern. He told us that the relationship was, quote, "not appropriate," that it was, quote, "wrong," and that it was, quote, "a critical lapse of judgment," and "a personal failure" on his part.

In addition, after seven months of denying that he had engaged in a sexual relationship with Ms. Lewinsky, the president admitted that his, quote, "public comments

43

about this matter gave a false impression." He said, "I misled people."

Mr. President, my immediate reaction to this statement that night it was delivered was deep disappointment and personal anger. I was disappointed because the president of the United States had just confessed to engaging in an extramarital affair with a young woman in his employ and to willfully deceiving the nation about his conduct. . . .

I was also angry because I was one of the many people who had said over the preceding seven months that if the president clearly and explicitly denies the allegations against him, then of course I believe him.

Well, since that Monday night, I have not commented on this matter publicly. I thought I had an obligation to consider the president's admissions more objectively, less personally, and to try to put them in a clearer perspective. . . .

But the truth is that after much reflection, my feelings of disappointment and anger have not dissipated, except now these feelings have gone beyond my personal dismay to a larger, graver sense of loss for our country, a reckoning of the damage that the president's conduct has done to the proud legacy of his presidency and ultimately an accounting of the impact of his actions on our democracy and its moral foundations.

The implications for our country are so serious that I feel a responsibility to my constituents in Connecticut as well as to my conscience to voice my concerns forthrightly and publicly, and I can think of no more appropriate place to do that than on this great Senate floor. . . .

Mr. President, I have come to this floor many times in the past to speak with my colleagues about the concerns which are so widely shared in this chamber and throughout the nation that our society's standards are sinking, that our common moral code is deteriorating, and that our public life is coarsening. In doing so, I have specifically criticized leaders of the entertainment industry for the way they have used the enormous influence they wield to weaken our common values.

And now, because the president commands at least as much attention and exerts at least as much influence on our collective consciousness as any Hollywood celebrity or television show, it is hard to ignore the impact of the misconduct the president has admitted to on our culture, on our character and on our children. . . .

In this case, the president apparently had extramarital relations with an employee half his age and did so in the workplace, in the vicinity of the Oval Office. Such behavior is not just inappropriate, it is immoral. And it is harmful, for it sends a message of what is acceptable behavior to the larger American family, particularly to our children, which is as influential as the negative messages communicated by the entertainment culture.

If you doubt that, just ask America's parents about the intimate and frequently unseemly sexual questions their young children have been asking them and discussing since the president's relationship with Ms. Lewinsky became public seven months ago. I have had many of those conversations with parents, particularly in Connecticut. And from them I conclude that parents across our country feel, much as I do, that something very sad and sordid has happened in American life when I cannot watch the news on television with my 10-year-old daughter anymore.

This unfortunately is all-too-familiar territory for America's families in today's anything-goes culture, where sexual promiscuity is treated as just another lifestyle choice with little risk of adverse consequences. It is this mindset that has helped to threaten the stability and integrity of the family, which continues to be the most important unit of civilized society, the place where we raise our children and teach them to be responsible citizens, to develop and nurture their personal and moral faculties. . . .

The president's relationship with Ms. Lewinsky not only contradicted the values he has publicly embraced over the last six years. It has, I fear, compromised his moral authority at a time when Americans of every political persuasion agree that the decline of the family is one of the most pressing problems we are facing.

Nevertheless, I believe that the president could have lessened the harm his relationship with Ms. Lewinsky has caused if he had acknowledged his mistake and spoken with candor about it to the American people shortly after it became public in January. But, as we now know, he chose not to do this.

This deception is particularly troubling because it was not just a reflexive and, in many ways, understandable human act of concealment to protect himself and his family from what he called the embarrassment of his own conduct when he was confronted with it in the deposition in the Jones case, but rather it was the intentional and premeditated decision to do so.

In choosing this path, I fear that the president has undercut the efforts of millions of American parents who are naturally trying to instill in our children the value of honesty. As most any mother and father knows, kids have a singular ability to detect double standards.

So we can safely assume that it will be that much more difficult to convince our sons and daughters of the importance of telling the truth when the most powerful man in the nation evades it. Many parents I have spoken with in Connecticut confirm this unfortunate consequence. . . .

Mr. President, I said at the outset that this was a very difficult statement to write and deliver.

That is true, very true. And it is true in large part because it is so personal and yet needs to be public, but also because of my fear that it will appear unnecessarily judgmental. I truly regret this. I know from the Bible that only God can judge people. The most that we can do is to comment without condemning individuals. And in this case, I have tried to comment on the consequences of the president's conduct on our country.

I know that the president is far from alone in the wrongdoing he has admitted. We as humans are all imperfect. We are all sinners. Many have betrayed a loved one and most have told lies.

Members of Congress have certainly been guilty of such behavior, as have some previous presidents. We try to understand -- we must try to understand the complexity and difficulty of personal relationships, which should give us pause before passing judgment on them. We all fall short of the standards our best values set for us. Certainly I do.

But the President, by virtue of the office he sought and was elected to, has traditionally been held to a higher standard. This is as it should be, because the American President, as I quoted earlier, is not just a one-man distillation of the American people but today the most powerful person in the world. And as such, the consequences of his misbehavior, even private misbehavior, are much greater than that of an average citizen, a CEO or even a senator. . . .

Let us as a nation honestly confront the damage that the president's actions over the last seven months have caused, but not to the exclusion of the good that his leadership has done over the past six years, nor at the expense of our common interest as Americans. And let us be guided by the conscience of the Constitution, which calls on us to place the common good above any partisan or personal interest, as we now, in our time, work together to resolve this serious challenge to our democracy.

I thank the chair. I thank my colleagues. And I yield the floor."

That was what Joe said. Vice President Gore said, "Bill Clinton is the greatest President in history." Ponder that one for a moment. "The greatest President in history."

I hear Hillary conjured up the spirit of George Washington, who upon being informed of the Clinton-Lewinsky situation said:

"Do what?"

The Presidential Butt and Other Observations

Now that President Clinton's term is about up, there's a great deal of speculation and discussion among the regulars at Abner's Bait & Tackle in Wewa about this President's future.

"You reck'n they gonna prosecute him?" George Bumgartner asked.

"Hell naw!" C.W. (I don't know his last name or what the initials stand for) fired back. "If'n that SOB, (I do know what those initials stand for) Al Gore gets elected, he'll pardon Clinton, and that'll be the end of it."

"Well, what if the Bush boy gets elected; what do you reck'n will happen then?" Willard Turnipseed asked.

"Then his last act in office will be to pardon hisself," C.W. responded.

"He cain't do that!" Charlie Johnson declared.

"The hell he cain't!," C.W. came right back. "He cain't be a draft dodger, a dope smoker, and a feller who'd stick his privates in a slop jar if'n it was still warm; and get elected President of these by God United States of America either can he? But he did," C.W. concluded.

Just then, Merlin Peterson and O'Dell Washington came through the screened door into the store. They were blacker'n hell. O'Dell was because he was born that way and Merlin was 'cause he was covered with soot. They have been inseparable since childhood and now were business partners.

"Afternoon boys," a chorus came from the group of philosophers.

49

"See you boys still trying to salvage some pulp from that St. Joe Fire," C.W. observed.

"Yes sir," O'Dell responded as he popped the cap off of his bottle of coke; "but at least we know that our country will stay free as long as you fellers are on the job."

"What sort of problems are y'all tacklin' today?" Merlin asked as he poured salted peanuts into his bottle of coke.

"C.W. thanks that Clinton is gonna pardon hisself," Charlie Johnson declared. Now Merlin, you know he cain't do that, can he?"

"Hell, I don't know," Merlin responded, "but I do know what I'd have done if that was my daughter," Merlin continued. "I would have called up O'Dell and asked him if he'd like to drive to Washington for a good old fashion butt whipping."

"I'll tell ya' what they should a' done," O'Dell responded. "They should a' cut down a couple of nice size bamboo poles and done a little caning."

"A little what?" the chorus sounded back in unison.

"Caning, you know; like what them folks in Singapore did to that rotten little rascal that spray-painted all of them cars. Yep, the Supreme Court ought to order that the President be taken right out there in the front yard of the White House. The Marine Corps Band would be playing "Hail to the Chief" and the Chief Justice would present Mr. Lewinsky with the official cane pole, and then read aloud the sentence of the Court. The Chief Justice would then declare: "Mr. President, pull down your pants and bend over" and then he'd say "Mr. Lewinsky, you may proceed with the caning . . . 40 licks less one."

"Eighty two gazillion photographers and reporters would be there, half of them zooming in on every pimple on the presidential rear end and the other half vividly capturing every grit of his teeth every time that pole reintroduced itself to that fat porker's butt. Then, the Chief Justice should present the pole to the President and have him commence beating the living hell out of Mr. Lewinsky, for suspecting his daughter was up to something like what she was up to, and then not doing a damned thing about it."

I think you're onto something O'Dell," C.W. declared while nodding his head in agreement. "Yep, I think you're on to something."

Sally Mae . . . I Owe You One

Joe and O'Dell raise some interesting concerns about explaining the President's strange sexual quandary to the ever inquiring minds of the children of our nation. I can't help but reminisce back to my own experience as a child trying to comprehend some of these baffling concepts . . .

I stood there at the plate. It was the bottom of the seventh (Dixie League equivalent to bottom of the ninth) and the score was tied 3 to 3. The stands were packed. The six, seven and eight year old boys sat on their bicycles along the outfield fence dreaming of the day they would make it here. The wind up and the pitch. A high hanging curve. The crowd stood to its feet. Everything went into slow motion. I connected and drove the ball deep into the left field corner and it was still rolling to the fence as I headed for second. I rounded second without looking at the location of the ball. I kept my eyes on the third base coach. The home-plate umpire had run down the line to position himself for the call. The third baseman straddled the bag with his waiting glove opened to the inside. The ball was on its way and I knew it. With outstretched arms, the third base coach pumped both hands downward several times. Hit the dirt! I lunged head first, diving for the bag. That precious bag.

"Saaaaafe!" came the call as the home-plate umpire threw one arm to the east and the other to the west. The crowd cheered for me, and the younger boys along the outfield fence slapped each other on their shoulders in excitement.

"What are you doing in there you little twit?" someone called out. Suddenly, in a single moment, the crowd vanished and I lay there in the dirt where the third base bag would be if this were actually a real game. I stood up quickly and began to brush the dirt off the front of my shirt and pants.

"You're not old enough to be in there," the voice called out again; "and I'm gonna tell."

It was Sally Mae Forehand. She was thirteen. I was suddenly eight again.

"I ain't hurting anything," I replied.

"Well, you're not old enough to be in there, and I'm going to tell."

"I will be old enough next year, and you'll still be just an ole girl."

"I won't tell if you'll come over here and give me a kiss," Sally Mae stated the terms of her blackmail as she puckered out her lips and made "smooching" noises at me.

I think I'm going to be sick, I thought. If she did tell the older boys that I was playing in here, there was the possibility that they might not believe her. After all, she is just a girl. Even if they did believe her, the worst I would get would be a sock in the eye or a kick in the stomach. Black eyes heal and as long as there was no damage to my internal organs, my stomach would eventually stop hurting, I thought.

"I would rather kiss a dog's butt than kiss you, Sally Mae," I yelled as I began picking up rocks and hurling them at her. Sally Mae rode away on her bicycle.

I began to walk home. I walked past the Philpot house just as Timothy was running out the back door. "Let's get up a game," he suggested.

"I have to go home and get my glove," I said. "I'll stop on the way and get Jim Beau," I offered.

"I'll go by and get Tommy and Russell and my brother Mark. They can each get someone else who can each get someone else," Timothy said. (He later made several millions dollars in a pyramid marketing business. I'm sure the idea started here.) Mark, Timothy's brother, was ten and a baseball legend. "We'll meet back at the park," I yelled as I ran toward home.

Within fifteen minutes or so, we had enough boys to field two teams. We were barely into the second inning when Sally Mae Forehand came riding up to the fence on her bicycle. Jim Beau Pendarvis started the chant, but it was quickly joined by everyone else.

"Sally Mae,
Sally Mae,
Two by four
Can't get through
The bathroom door."

All the boys laughed, but Sally Mae seemed unmoved. She was like a black widow spider, seeking out her next victim. Eugene Primrose rode up on his bicycle with his glove hooked onto the right handle bar.

"All positions are filled," Mark Philpot advised from the pitcher's mound. Sally Mae rode over next to Eugene and they disappeared behind the closed concession stand. Everyone snickered. Everyone except Mark. He threw the next pitch and struck out David Maples swinging. We came in from the field to bat.

Sally Mae and Eugene were still behind the concession stand. We all snickered more.

"Fat girls can move their tongues better than a bus station queer," Mark reported.

"A what?" I thought. My curiosity couldn't take it. "What's a bus station queer?" I blurted out.

"Don't you know nothing? Are you an ignoramus?" Mark asked me. He wasn't really expecting a reply.

At that very moment, Sally Mae and Eugene reappeared from behind the concession stand and walked toward their bicycles which were still leaning against the fence. This time Russell started it . . . but the chorus joined in just the same:

"Eugene and Sally May sitting in a tree
K-I-S-S-I-N-G
First comes love
Then comes marriage
Here comes Eugene with a baby carriage."

Eugene's face turned tomato red and he jumped on his bicycle and quickly rode away. Sally Mae just stood there smiling like a bird dog eating green persimmons.

"Revell," Mark began. Real life baseball players always call people by their last name. It's a rule. "A bus station queer is somebody that don't like girls," he continued.

I must be a bus station queer for sure, I thought, but at least Mark didn't know it. His own brother Timothy was a bus station queer too, but I wasn't about to squeal on him. I looked around at the other boys, Jim Beau, Tommy, Russell and Zack . . . all bus station queers. Mark didn't know it, but he couldn't have spit in that ball field without hitting at least one bus station queer.

Then an agonizing heart pounding fear hit me. Sally Mae knew, but would she tell? After all, it hadn't been more than a hour and a half ago that I had pelted her with rocks and told her that I'd rather kiss a dog's butt, than kiss her. Sally Mae turned and looked straight at me. My heart froze. She puckered up her lips and made that "smooching" sound. Then she just turned and rode away.

Thanks Sally Mae, I owe you one.

Fixing

I have a fascination with words. I particularly like them when they are placed on paper. They may provoke a gamut of emotions or recollections or inquisitive thought. I like the feel and the smell of books. I touch the words and sometimes allow them to touch me.

Until recently, the closest booksellers to my house were Waldenbooks or B. Dalton, each a forty five minute drive. I know that Amazon.com is a lot closer, and although I have bought books from them (like the Hebrew-English Tanakh), I generally like to touch a book before I buy it.

In more recent times, Books-A-Million opened a store in Destin, a mere eighteen minutes from here to there. I have heard that Barnes & Noble is opening a store even closer to me. I'm sure that I will pass many hours there.

Today, I went to Destin, to the Books A Million. There's even a "Joe Muggs" coffee shop in the bookstore. I overheard two well dressed ladies talking between sips of their cappuccino. From the conversation, I gathered that they were from the small South Georgia town of Camilla.

"How old is your Charles, now?" the one asked.

"Why, Charles is 9 and 'fixing' to enter the third grade," the other responded.

"Fixing," I thought. There's a word I haven't spoken or heard spoken in that context in many years. It's a perfectly good word and one that I used quite regularly in my early childhood. That is, until some moron from New Jersey or some other such hellish place asked, upon hearing me say it, "Is it broken?" I knew that one may set about "fixing" something that was broken, but this was a different use of the word altogether. It had nothing to do with repairs. Thereafter, every time I heard "fixing" used in that context, I thought of that ignoramus' question, "Is it broken?"

Eventually the word, at least in the non-repair sense of it, simply passed from my vocabulary. I don't know why I allowed that to happen. No one, especially one whose personal vocabulary limits his own use of "fixing" to a single definition, should ever be allowed to strip another's more advanced vocabulary of any word or use of that word.

"Why, Charles is 9, and he's fixing to enter the third grade."

I don't care if everyone in New Jersey is incapable of understanding the information that was conveyed by that response. I did, and I didn't need an interpreter. I knew there was nothing broken in that situation. It is used merely as another proper and legitimate definition of the word. It means: "to prepare."

It's like running out on the porch at your grandmother's house and telling your cousin, "Grandma's fixing turnip greens with pepper sauce and cornbread." Neither the food, nor any ingredients therein (except for the egg in the cornbread) is broken—it is merely being prepared.

"Charles is fixing to enter the third grade," means simply that he is preparing to do so. Charles isn't broken, and the school's not broken, but if I could find that ignoramus from New Jersey, his nose would be. I would put forth the effort to locate that scoundrel, but I'm hungry, and I hear that Elmo's has all the crawfish you can eat for

$6.95, so I think I'll go. Yes, that's exactly what I'm <u>fixing</u> to do, and I <u>cain't</u> wait to get there.

The Joe and Dick Show

If you missed the vice-presidential debate last night between Senator Joe Lieberman and Secretary Dick Cheney, trust me, you didn't miss anything. The whole thing amounted to nothing more than jaw muscle exercise. I have therefore decided to enter the debate myself, so here goes;

SHAW: I thought it would be colder out here, but this is comfortable. From historic Danville, Kentucky, good evening and welcome to this year's only vice presidential debate sponsored by the Commission on Presidential Debates. I'm Bernard Shaw of CNN, moderator.

Tonight we come to you from Newlin Hall in the Norton Center for the Arts on the campus of Centre College. To President John Rousch, the faculty here, students and community leaders statewide, we thank you for hosting this debate.

The only candidate that matters in this debate is Ken Revell, a columnist, a lawyer, and a part time a goat farmer from Santa Rosa Beach, Florida. The commission, the candidate and his campaign staff have agreed to the following rules: I ask the questions. He gives the answers.

This audience has been told no disruptions will be tolerated. A prior coin toss as well as the fact that he is the only candidate that matters here tonight has determined that the first question will go to Ken Revell.

SHAW: Mr. Revell, few hard-working Americans would base their well being on bonuses they hope to get five or 10 years from now. Why do you and your opponent, predict surpluses you cannot possibly guarantee to pay for your proposed programs?

REVELL: It's just a wild ass guess, Bernie. Nobody knows for sure.

SHAW: You just picked the numbers out of the air?

REVELL: Well, at least I didn't conjure up Eleanor Roosevelt to help me.

SHAW: What if it falls short of your projected figures?

REVELL: Actually Bernie, I have already thought about that one. If the numbers fall short, we'll hire Ed McMahan to send out a mailing to everyone in the world promising them that they have won $50 million and all they have to do is mail in ten bucks to collect their loot. Of course no one will actually win anything, but Ed swears that we can drum up $1.5 trillion or so with the scam. He's so sure of it, he's willing to work on commission.

SHAW: Mr. Revell, you alluded to problems in public education. There's no magic bullet, and this question to you: No magic bullets to solve the problems of public education, but what's the next best solution?

REVELL: What kind of convoluted run on question is that Bernie? I take it that you learned grammar in the public schools.

Anyway, I disagree with you about there being no magic bullets to solve the problems of public education. The problems are:

> No discipline
> Lack of respect
> Lack of motivation among the students, and

A Democratic party with its collective head so far up the butt of the NEA that they can't even see the problem, much less form a solution.

The solution is "vouchers." The poorest family in America will then be able to remove their children from an unproductive school send them to the finest most productive schools in America.

SHAW: Wouldn't that strip money from public schools and destroy them?

REVELL: Bernie, you are assuming that there are no good public schools and that's just not the case. Vouchers would introduce a level of competition for excellence among all schools, public and private. The ones that cain't hang with the big dogs should get off the porch!

SHAW: Follow up question. Why are you so sure that the voucher system will work to better educate our nation's children?

REVELL: My uncle Jean-Thomas Revell had a daughter, Joyce Marie. Now Joyce Marie was a bright child, but the rascal just could not seem to get her math studies down. In frustration, Uncle Jean-Thomas sent the child to the St. Teresa's Catholic School. Now, Joyce Marie, she came home that first day and went straight to her room and studied her math books until she was called out for dinner. She ate and went straight back to the books. The same thing occurred the next day, and every day after that. At the end of the term, Joyce Marie came home and tossed her report card, still sealed in an envelope, down on the kitchen table and went straight to her room to study. Uncle Jean-Thomas opened the envelope and looked at the report card. Math: A+. He went directly to Joyce Marie's room where she was diligently studying. "Joyce Marie," he said, " I got to know. Was it de nuns, de curriculum or de other students? What made de difference?" Joyce Marie said, "Papa, dat first day, when you dropped me off dere, at dat school; I went in de front door and I seen where de done nailed dat man to dat big plus sign. I said to myself, 'oh, Joyce Marie, dese people, dey mean bidness.'"

Bernie, we need a school system that means business and if the government can't compete, then they should get out of the business.

SHAW: Gentleman, this is the 21st century, yet on average an American working woman in our great nation earns 75 cents for each dollar earned by a working male. What do you, a male, propose to do about it. Mr. Gore has suggested the Equal Pay Act, which would allow women to sue their employers over their pay. What would you do?

REVELL: Nothing.

SHAW: What?!

REVELL: Nothing.

SHAW: You mean you would do nothing?

REVELL: Yes.

SHAW: What kind of answer is that?

REVELL: A truthful one. Bernie, I think you've been hanging around these politicians too much. You look a little blue around the gills. Maybe you should take a vacation.

SHAW: Mr. Revell, do you not care that women are earning less?

REVELL: Of course I do Bernie. If a male business owner pays a superior employee less money merely because she is female, that business owner is an idiot, and that woman will probably end up either owning his business or driving him out of business when she opens a competing one. Except for salaries paid from public funds, it ain't the government's business. Believe me Bernie, the woman that feels comfortable today with the government sticking its nose in her bosses business will live to rue that day. She'll think differently when the government comes after her for not hiring enough elderly, slovic, bisexual, gothic, mustached, underweight employees. That, Bernie, is when a Democrat becomes a Republican.

SHAW: Would you support the effort of House Republicans who want legislation to restrict distribution of the abortion drug RU 486?

REVELL: Yes.

SWAW: Any explanation?

REVELL: Do you need one Bernie?

SHAW: I think so.

REVELL: If this thing goes through it will replace the hormonal birth control pill which merely adjusts the female fertility cycle. RU 486 is not a birth control pill. It is a chemical abortion. It will not take Hillary & Co. three weeks to start "pushing" the pills on school playgrounds. Trust me on that one Bernie.

SHAW: Of course, this question is for you Mr. Revell. If Yugoslavia's Slobodan Milosevic prevails, notwithstanding the election results, would you support his overthrow?

REVELL: I would ask the President to direct the Joint Chiefs to immediately put together an elite 9 man squad—3 each from the Navy Seals, Army Rangers and Marine Special Forces. We are one country again boys, get used to it. Slobodan, I hope you can sleep with one eye open!

SHAW: Mr. Revell, this question to you. Once again in the Middle East, peace talks on the one hand, deadly confrontations on the other, and the flash point, Jerusalem, and then there's Syria. Is United States policy what it should be?

REVELL: No.

SHAW: Would you like to elaborate?

REVELL: Make no bones about it Bernie; as long as Arafat's Fatah, the Hamas and the militant Islamic Jihad maintain as their ultimate objective – the elimination of Israel from the face of the earth, there can be no peace. As long as they teach their children that the very existence of Israel is a "catastrophe" and encourage the intifadas to continue – there can be no future permanent peace. Our government believes that the Islamic Jihad is responsible for the bombing of the U.S. embassies in Tanzania and Kenya. I suppose liberals think we should give them Arizona in exchange for their terrorism. Bull. Give 'em Newark.

SHAW: Follow up question. Mr. Revell, what would you do to quell the violence in the middle east and bring about peace between Jews and Arabs?

REVELL: First I would get the CIA to dress up like Arafat and kill a couple of members of every street gang in Newark.

SHAW: How would that quell violence in the Middle East?

REVELL: Let me finish, Bernie. We would leave behind dozens of posters depicting the likeness of Yasser Arafat and declaring him the main homey of our new rival gang. Next I would offer all gangs a free trip to Israel under the pretense of learning guerilla fighting tactics from elite Israeli forces. Of course, when they all arrived there wouldn't be any such training. They would all be mad as hell, so we would dump them off outside the Hamas headquarters. When they saw posters of Arafat everywhere . . . well, see Bernie, I just solved two problems.

SHAW: This question is for you, Mr. Revell.

If Iraq's president, Saddam Hussein, were found to be developing weapons of mass destruction, Governor Bush has said he would, quote, "Take him out." Would you agree with such a deadly policy?

REVELL: Saddam, do you remember Slobodan? I hope you're better at sleeping with one eye open than he was. Good luck.

SHAW: Mr. Revell, this question is to you. Many experts are forecasting continuing chaotic oil prices on the world market. Wholesale natural gas prices here in our country are leaping, then there are coal and electricity. Have previous Republican and Democratic Congresses and administrations, including this one, done their job to protect the American people?

REVELL: No.

SHAW: Would you like to elaborate, ah; Follow up question, Mr. Revell. What would you do to decrease our reliance on natural gas?

REVELL: Catching on, ain't you Bernie?

SHAW: I think so.

REVELL: I would put a humungous rubber balloon over Washington D. C. I would use the hot air collected to drive a steam plant on the Potomac. We could supply power from D.C. to Baltimore. We may even finance a Balloon for every State Capitol. Imagine that Bernie, the hot air is already paid for, we're just putting it to use.

SHAW: Mr. Revell, you sponsored a bill that said no to oil and gas exploration off the Florida Gulf Coast, your home state. However, you co-sponsored a bill that said yes to drilling the Arctic National Wildlife Refuge. Your explanation.

REVELL: How many Americans spend the better part of their year looking forward to a vacation in the Arctic Refuge? Come on Bernie, don't act like a moron.

SHAW: With all do respect, Mr. Revell, do you not care for the residents of the Arctic National Wildlife Refuge?

REVELL: Of course I do Bernie. Haven't you heard that Bullwinkle and Rocky J. Squirrel moved there after the Presidential debate Tuesday. Too many questions about the exact nature of their relationship; or so I have heard.

SHAW: Mr. Revell, this question is for you. Washington is a cauldron of political bickering and partisanship. The

American people, gentleman, have had enough. How would you elevate political discourse and purpose.

REVELL: I say we freeze water on the floor of the house and senate. We hire Wayne Gretsky. When somebody gets out of line, Gretsky will skate up to him or her and bust them in the head with his hockey stick and if they're still conscious, they have to sit in a penalty box with Ralph Nader for two minutes. The bickering will stop within a week.

SHAW: Ken Revell, you are black for this question. Imagine yourself an African-American. You become the target of racial profiling, either while walking or driving.

REVELL: Can I be the black Vice President of the United States or do you want me to be a street thug who's packing a 9 millimeter or just an innocent middle aged upper class black citizen like yourself, Bernie? What the hell kind of question is this anyway? Where's Jim Lehrer? He didn't have a car accident on the way over here did he?

SHAW: I don't think so.

REVELL: Tell the truth Bernie, you didn't write these questions did you?

SHAW: No response.

REVELL: First of all Bernie, we all know that if I was black, unless I was Colin Powell, then I wouldn't be the Vice Presidential nominee of either one of the two major parties, so I wouldn't be standing here, trying my best to answer this stupid question. That is the sad truth, Bernie. It's especially sad when we've got a man like J.C. Watts in Congress. I'll assume that what you intended on asking me is; (1) what do I think about law enforcement racism?; and (2) if I was the Vice President of the United States, what would I do about it?

First, racism in general is straight from the pit of hell. In America we should never attempt to punish thought. Sure there will always be the David Dukes and the Al Sharptons, but personal beliefs, whether concealed in secret or espoused in public, must remain free if we are to remain free.

Bernie, in order that you can understand where I'm coming from about this racist thing, I want to give you these three columns that I wrote long before this campaign ever began.

SHAW: At the moderator's discretion; and because we're about an hour ahead of schedule, and because I have to go to the bathroom, we will break while I read these columns into the record . . .

Isabel, Me & Mikey
Makes Three

We stood there looking into the crib at my newborn baby brother. "He sure is small, ain't he Isabel?"

"Chile, that baby ain't small; he was born at better'n nine pounds. That ain't small."

"Well, he looks small to me, I said."

"You're almost four, so naturally he'd look small compared to you. He'll grow; you'll see."

He did.

Two and a half years later, I started grammar school at Magnolia Elementary. My first day was sort of scary, and when it was over, I ran all the way to the railroad tracks, down which Uncle Raymond would sometimes drive his train and blow the horn and wave at me as I played in a nearby field. I was in familiar territory now, and I slowed to a fast walk. When I got to the edge of the lot where the big pump house sat, I could see the corner of the street on which our house was located. On that corner stood Isabel, holding my baby brother in one arm and a rope leash in the other hand. Attached to the leash was my dog, Candy.

They had come out to greet me. I felt like a war hero coming home. I had conquered the first day of the first grade.

I started running as fast as I could and when I got to them, I wrapped my arms tightly around Isabel's leg. She set my little brother down on his feet in the grass and handed him the leash that was attached to the dog. She picked me up and looked straight into my eyes. She didn't say a word, but I could see tears in hers. She hugged me tight and kissed my face. Her cheeks were fat and black, and I pressed my little pink lips square on them. I kissed her cheeks several times.

"I love you," I said.

"I love you too," she responded as she placed my feet back onto the lawn.

My little brother and I ran for the house with Candy in tow. I was safe now. I was home. Isabel was about five foot three and pushing two hundred sixty. She waddled behind us.

You boys, wash your hands and get on in that kitchen, so we can eat, Isabel called out to us as we ran ahead of her. My little brother informed me in broken two year old english that they had not eaten. They were waiting on me.

"They fed us at school" I said.

"Chile, I'm gone put some meat on them bones of yours if it's the last thing I do before I go home to Jesus," Isabel answered.

She spooned out her beef stew and cut the cornbread. The three of us sat there just as it had always been, before I started school. She reached out her hands—one toward each of us. We knew the routine. I put my tiny left hand in her hand and gripped my brother's left with my right. She reached across the table and held his other one.

"God is Great,
God is Good,
Let us thank him
For our Food,
By his hands,
We are fed,
Give us Lord,

Our daily bread . . . Amen."

Isabel had taught me the blessing and since I was the oldest male among the three of us, it was always my responsibility to bless the food. I'm sure the National Organization for women would not have approved, but I know what Isabel would say, "I ain't studying them, anyway."

After we ate, she put my brother down for his nap. We watched "Dark Shadows." I can still hear the scary music from that program. I crawled into her lap.

"Isabel, when I grow up and have children—will you come and keep them safe?" I asked.

"Lord knows I will. You know I will."

"I love you Isabel."

"I love you too, baby."

Niggah Luvah

"You're supposed to brush up and down, not side to side," I instructed my little brother as I spat in the bathroom sink.

"I don't like up and down," he explained.

"Teeth doctors don't care what you like or don't like. You just have to brush like they say."

"What if I don't brush up and down?" he asked.

"If you don't, they have a giant drill, sort of like a jack hammer and they'll pry open your mouth with a crow bar and drill out your teeth."

His eyes opened wide as he screamed, "Iiisssaaabbbeeell!"

"What is it baby?"

"Do teeth doctors have drills that they use to drill teeth?"

"Yes baby. You keep your teeth brushed good and they won't be drilling in your mouth. You children hurry up, your breakfast is getting cold."

Isabel left the doorway.

"I told you they had a drill."

"Well, she didn't say nothing about a crow bar."

"You keep brushing your teeth side to side and you'll see that crow bar when they pry open your mouth."

"I'll brush my teeth up and down from now on," my brother conceded.

We finished brushing and rinsed our mouths with water.

As we started out of the bathroom, Michael looked at me with pleading eyes and asked, "You ain't gone tell

74

that I ever brushed my teeth side to side are you? I won't do it anymore, I promise."

"No, I won't tell," I reassured him.

This was my second day in the first grade and no sooner had we gathered in front of the schoolhouse to await the "beginning bell," when Nedd Sapp started screaming at me. "Niggah Luvah!" Ned was nine years old and still in the first grade. He was meaner than hell, and everyone was afraid of him. He always wore black boots and a sharpened pencil stuck in the gap between his skull and his left ear. "I saw you kissing that big black niggah woman yesterday," he advised.

My eyes got wide. He could beat me up right here in front of everybody. I was terrified. What if he killed me? I trembled and my voice quivered as I said the only word that I could muster at the time . . . "What?"

"You heard me 'Niggah Luvah,' If I ever see you kissing your big fat 'niggah mammy' ever again, I'm gone stomp your butt in the dirt."

When the final bell rang that day, I ran and ran and ran toward home. I got to the railroad tracks, but I didn't slow down. I did look behind me every thirty or forty seconds, but I just kept running.

I saw Isabel, my brother Michael and my dog Candy, all standing on the corner waiting for me. I ran full blast until I got to them. She picked me up.

"What's wrong with you baby?" Isabel asked.

I couldn't hold back the tears and I started to cry. She hugged me and I tried to stop crying and I began to sniffle.

"Isabel?"

"Yes baby."

"What's a Niggah Luvah?"

For the first time in my life, I saw the soul of a human being depart the eyes of its host.

I'm sure that she knew that I would eventually be subjected to those kind of thoughts, but she probably had hoped that it wouldn't occur so soon. "We'll talk about that during Michael's nap," she said, as she stood me on my feet without kissing me. We all walked home rather quickly.

I blessed the food.

We ate.

Me and my little brother talked.

Isabel didn't mutter a word.

As soon as we finished eating, she put Michael in bed for his afternoon nap.

She came back to the living-room and sat down next to me.

"Chile," she began, "this world is full of mean people, but I don't want you to be afraid of them. I also don't want you to be stupid when you have dealings with them." She was doing her best to explain, but the mind of a six year old needs clarity.

"But Isabel, what is a Niggah Luvah?"

"Do you see that my skin is darker than yours?"

"Yes."

"I am a Negro and that's why my skin is this color, but some mean people will call me a niggah."

"I have freckles on my skin. Am I part Negro?"

"No baby, you are Caucasian. It means that your kin folks come from a different place than mine."

"I reckon we wouldn't be blood kin?"

"No, we ain't blood kin."

"Isabel?"

"Yes baby."

"Even if we ain't blood kin, I still love you."

"I love you too, baby."

I felt better. I crawled up into her lap and we still caught the last half of Dark Shadows."

Learning About the Civil Rights Movement in School

The next day, I walked to school slowly, because I was afraid to go there. I hid in the bushes until the beginning bell rang. It seemed like it took forever, but it finally rang and I ran to the classroom and sat down. I tried not to look at Ned Sapp, but it's hard not to look at someone who wants to stomp your butt into the dirt. I tried glancing out the corner of my eye. Maybe his preacher had come by his house last night and talked to him about love and kindness. Maybe he had seen the error of his ways. Why, he probably didn't want to stomp my butt into the dirt anymore, I thought.

I turned and looked back at him. He squinted his eyes at me as he stuck out his "pointing" finger and slowly drew it across his throat. He was going to murder me for sure.

I was terrified. I needed to go to the bathroom, but I didn't dare ask permission to go. If I did, he would also "need" to go and he would kill me in the bathroom. I just held it.

The bell rang for recess, and everyone else ran out to swing or climb on the monkey bars.

"Miss Cooper, I don't feel so good, can I just stay in here with you?" I asked.

"You could, but I have a meeting. If you're sick, I can call your mother or father to come and pick you up."

They would ask too many questions, I thought. My mother would feel my forehead and ask me to open my mouth and say "ah."

78

"There's nothing wrong with you," she would know immediately.

"Naw, I'll be alright," I said.

"Go on outside, but don't get overheated," Miss Cooper instructed.

I walked outside on legs that felt like spaghetti noodles.

The boys were all at the far end of the schoolyard playing softball. The girls were swinging on a giant metal swingset. I walked over to the girls and sat in a swing.

"I ain't feeling too good," I said, explaining my presence. They seemed to accept the explanation. About that time, Ned Sapp spotted me and came walking up to where I sat. I got up, ready to run. "I told you what I'd do if I caught you kissing your niggah mammy again, didn't I?" Ned reminded me of his threat.

"But Isabel ain't no mammy," I said. "She's a Negro. Her kin folks ain't from around here."

"Shut up, Niggah Luvah."

"I didn't' kiss her again," I pleaded for mercy. "I just hugged her."

"You dirty, rott'n, stink'n Niggah Luvah, I'm gonna stomp your butt in the dirt."

"Ned, how about if I promise to never kiss her again. I'll only hug her, but I won't kiss her," I proposed.

He just stared at me.

"You want to shake on it," my voice quivered as I held out my right hand to seal the deal.

Ned reached up to his ear and snatched the sharpened pencil from it. He then stabbed it into my hand just above where my middle finger connected. I looked at my hand, the pencil slowly rocking back and forth, still embedded in my flesh. I looked up at Ned. For some

79

bizarre reason, it didn't hurt. I reached out with my left hand and pulled the pencil from my flesh.

Betsy Eubanks took off running for the schoolhouse. "Miss Cooper! Miss Cooper!"

I raised my hand and threw the pencil on the ground at Ned's feet. He flinched and every boy in the schoolyard saw it. He was later beaten up by a seven year old.

I didn't see much of Ned after that. I'm sure he was still there, but I wasn't "studying him, nor anything he had to say" after that.

After 37 years, that pencil mark is still there, and not just in my flesh, either.

The Joe and Dick Show, Part II

SHAW: Good evening again, from historic Danville Kentucky and this year's only Vice Presidential Debate sponsored by the commission on Presidential Debates. Where were we?

REVELL: I was answering the question what I would do as Vice President to stop government-based racism.

SHAW: Please Proceed.

REVELL: Government racism as expressed through the "police power" is different. It can never be acceptable nor tolerated. The V.P. presides as the president of the Senate. I would use that position to demand that all racial profiling among federal law enforcement be made statutorily unlawful. The V.P. should have the ear of the President and I would strongly request that the Pres. nominate, and the Senate confirm, an Attorney General committed to the elimination of racism in federal law enforcement. I would also use the office to encourage all state governors and state legislatures to do the same. I would also try to dismantle the Democrats' longstanding policy of paternal racism— putting black people on welfare and quota reservations. It strips dignity and subserviates people to the Great White Father – Washington, D.C. People, whatever color they are, need to be treated equally. *Poor people*, regardless of race, need to be helped and encouraged out of poverty and off of government "relief" programs—not made dependent upon them. Other than that, education, vouchers, and my street gang export plan, there just ain't a hellava lot more you can do, Bernie.

SHAW: Mr. Revell, sexual orientation. Should a male who loves a male and a female who loves a female have all – all – the Constitutional rights enjoyed by every American citizen?

REVELL: Bernie, is this like the commercial where two guys are fishing off a dock and the one looks at the other, his dad, brother, or cousin, or something like that, and says, "I love you man," and the other one looks back and says, "you still can't have my beer." . . . ? Is that what you're talking about here, Bernie?

SHAW: No.

REVELL: I was afraid of that. Wait a second, Bernie, do you mean to tell me that you are asking me about a grown man who enjoys . . .

SHAW: Well . . .

SHAW: Time. Next question.

SHAW: It occurs to me that your moderator has committed a booboo. I asked the racial profiling question of you; you responded. And then I asked the sexual orientation question of you. I should not have done that in terms of rotation. Gentleman, I apologize.

REVELL: Don't worry about it, Bernie, they were both stupid questions.

SHAW: Mr. Revell, Vice President of the United States of America, what would you bring to the job that your opponent wouldn't.

REVELL: Honesty. That would be a pleasant change wouldn't it, Bernie?

SHAW: And because of my booboo, I'm going to direct this question again to Mr. Revell.

Have you noticed a contradiction or hypocritical shift by your opponent on positions and issues since he was nominated.

REVELL: No. I stopped hanging around him once he hooked up with Gore and grew that forked tongue.

SHAW: Gentlemen, now closing statements. A prior coin toss has determined that you begin, Mr. Revell.

REVELL: This country pits self interest against self sacrifice. When I was a kid, parents always said, "I want you to have it better than I did." We don't say that anymore. We have become a nation in which the Democrats have pitted the well-being of the next generation against the economic security of today's elderly. Welfare programs against military preparedness. It was not a Republican who first said this, but I think it's worth repeating, "Ask not what your country can do for you, but what you can do for your country." If we don't do that, we may lose this wonderful experiment; America.

(APPLAUSE)

SHAW: Well, you hear the appreciation HERE. And our thanks also to Centre College, the community of Danville, and of course the Bluegrass State, Kentucky.

For the Commission on Presidential Debates, I'm Bernard Shaw. Good night from Danville, Kentucky.

Say it Ain't So Joe ...
Say It Ain't So

The year was 1920 and eight members of the Chicago White Sox were barred for life from organized major league baseball. They each played some part in throwing the 1919 World Series. The players were Chick Gandil, Swede Risberg, Eddie Cicotte, Lefty Williams, Happy Felsch, Fred McMullin, Buck Weaver and of course the immortal Shoeless Joe Jackson. Shoeless Joe admitted that he took the money, but claimed that he double crossed the gamblers and played his best. His story actually holds water; Jackson hit .375 for the series with 12 hits and 6 RBIs. He committed no errors.

Today, I was thinking about Shoeless Joe and the blacksox of 1919. I'm not sure why? There's a movement, you know, to get Shoeless Joe reinstated to major league baseball. Why? So he can be inducted into the MLB Hall of Fame at Cooperstown. I thought about that prospect and my initial inclination was; it's been over eighty years and Shoeless Joe was a great player. Why not give him a reprieve? Yea, I know, he admits that he took the money. Is there no place in baseball for "grace?"

Last night, I listened to the Vice Presidential debates and I saw a man that I greatly respected—another Joe—take the money. Does it really matter that he does the right thing if or when he gets into office? I don't think so. Whether Shoeless Joe actually threw the game is of little consequence to me now. Taking the money—that's enough. Say it ain't so Joe; please say it ain't so.

IV

Muster the Troops—There's Genocide in Bosnia

The Deep South ... It's In My Bones

It seems a lot smaller today than the first time I stood here, thirty years and seven months ago. That was the first time I would stand in this very spot, but it was not to be the last. It's a lot warmer too. A lot warmer. The heat index is near 110 degrees, although the actual temperature is only about 100. A couple of feet in front of me lie the remains of my mother. To the immediate right of her lies her sister, who died in infancy. From the looks of this place, that seems to have been a common thing back then. To her right is my grandfather, and a few feet away are my great grandparents. In fact, it seems that nearly everyone here is in one way or another related to me, by blood or by marriage. I suppose the only way to get here is to be born here, or to be begotten of people who were.

This is deep south—just a stone's throw from the Florida-Georgia border.

Behind me is the Hopeful Baptist Church. The land for the church and cemetery were given by my great great great grandfather to be used for these purposes. I wonder if he ever had a thought that on some July day, a hundred and fifty plus years later, when the gnats were thick and the sun was hot, his great great great grandson would stand here in this place and remember a mother who loved him so. Remember a grandfather who taught him how to throw a curve ball and who bought him the first pair of "overalls" he would ever wear, although not in that order. Remember the story of his mother's birth in which his grandfather, her father, had hitched up a team of mules to a wagon and driven them to the nearest doctor. By the time he returned to the farm with the physician, his daughter, Sara Ann, had, with the help of a mid-wife, already arrived. She would be the last of this line to be born on a farm. We placed her remains here a little over a year and a half ago.

It was on the one year anniversary of the birth of her twin granddaughters. She was so proud of them. "I have some news for y'all," I said. It seemed all right to be talking to them like that. I would never try to talk to Eleanor Roosevelt like that, but then I didn't know Eleanor Roosevelt and Eleanor Roosevelt didn't know me. Besides, she wouldn't really care about my news anyway.

"In just a few weeks, I'm going to have a son; his name is Joshua Caleb," I said.

"That's a lovely name," my mother would have replied, as my grandfather quietly agreed. "What prompted you to select that name?" my mother would certainly ask.

My grandfather would not ask that; as he would be preoccupied with locating a store that offered near infant sized "overalls" in this year 2000.

"Read Numbers 13," I responded.

"I will certainly do that," she would assure me. "I'm just tickled pink for you," my mother would add.

"I can't wait to meet him," my grandfather would have said. Grandfathers always talk like that you know.

"I'm going to go tell Daddy, I know he'll be excited too," I said.

"You know he will," they would both have agreed.

"I love you," I said.

"I love you too," my mother would respond. Then she would say, "you look thin. Are you eating enough?"

"I'm eating plenty."

"Well, you look thin to me."

"I'm fine."

"Take care of yourself son, that boy needs you."

"I will mom."

"Please do. Come over here and let me hug you," she would say. She would hug me long and hard.

"Now, go over there and hug your 'DeDaddy.'" My grandfather would hug me next, not so long, but harder.

I walked back to the truck and began to pull out of the cemetery and I drove off the edge of the small drive and straight into a ditch. The pickup fell nose first into the ditch and the rear wheels were sticking straight up into the air. I got out and looked. "Oh brother! How did you manage to do this?" I asked myself.

Within seconds, two farmers; one in his early twenties and the other in his late forties, each stopped. The younger one backed his truck up to mine and without saying a word, pulled out a chain and began attaching it to each of the trucks. The older one pulled up beside me and asked, "who are your folks here, son?" I told him and he looked at the younger man and the younger one looked back and smiled. "Younger" pulled forward and my truck raised its nose from the ditch in what appeared to be an effortless exercise. By now they were both standing beside me.

"Well cousin, how did you manage to do this?" the older one asked.

"Just as I was about to leave, I got something in my eye, and ran off in the ditch," I explained. The three of us stood there in silence, staring at the ground for several seconds. The younger farmer broke the still and the silence with a light kick at the ground and said, "I know what you mean cuz, exactly what you mean."

Muster the Troops—There's Genocide in Bosnia

October 3, 2000; my son, Joshua Caleb, was born at 12:20 a.m. today. It was the most amazing thing that I have ever experienced in my life. If you think there is no God, then you have never witnessed the birth of your child. My wife and I cried as our little "Governor Boudreaux" came out of her body.

As he began to emerge, I could see the top of his head. I could see his hair. As his head emerged I noted that he was face down. Dr. Moraczewski (pronounced Morcheski), gently lifted his head and he began to gurgle as if he were gasping for breath.

Within a couple of seconds, the good doctor suctioned the fluid from the little guy's mouth and nostrils and he began to breath, cough and cry. The rest of his body then slipped on out. Dr. Moraczewski cradled him and cleaned him. He was still connected by the umbilical cord to his mother. His eyes were open. He was breathing, gurgling and crying. I chose not to cut the cord. He was placed on my wife's chest. She looked at me and whispered, "He's our little one flesh." His eyes were open wide, like a little kid at a circus.

They wheeled my wife off to another room and handed the "Governor Boudreaux" to me. I held him carefully. I cried. I took him to the nursery where he was weighed and checked. "8 pounds 3 ounces, and he's perfect," the nurse announced. I left the nursery and went into the stairwell where I was all alone. I cried again.

92

When did Joshua Caleb become a human being with a life worth protecting? I am asking you? Was it only when I could see the hair on his head? When his head came out? Or maybe when he started to cry? Perhaps you think it was when his entire body was out of his mother? Or maybe when the umbilical cord was cut? Does his race determine when he became human? His sex? Or the social, financial or political standing of his parents? Does he only become human when he can vote?

Is an unloved baby human? Or do you think he only became a human being when two people began to love him?

That happened a long time before today.

If you have personally witnessed the birth of a child and you remain a proponent of partial birth abortion, you should be confined—somewhere. You are a danger to a civilized society. What does this have to do with the Presidential election, you ask?

Al Gore says that he will appoint Supreme Court Justices who will assert that a person has the Constitutionally protected right to stab a partially born baby in the back of the head with a pair of scissors, suck out his or her brains until his or her head collapses and then drag the dead limp body from its mother. Bush says he will bring a stop to this killing. And that's all I have to say about that.

Uncle Buddy

He was a kind and gentle-man. He was a gentleman. He was old and a great teller of family tales. It came easy to him. He had lived it. I thought about him today. My birthday is tomorrow—August 18. His was today, somewhere in the late 1880's.

"I'm not old," he would tell me, "I'm only one day older than you!"

He spoke of family members who had departed this world. He told me about his "Aunt Lou." He described what she looked like, the clothes that she often wore and told me when she died and where she was buried. "Aunt Lou would be your great great great grandmother," he said.

Imagine that for a moment. My great great great grandmother. Louisiana Virginia was little more than a name to me, but this man, Uncle Buddy, had seen her, touched her, smelled her and had been cradled in her arms. She had probably changed his diapers—in a previous century. She was more to him than a name on somebody's pedigree. She was a living, breathing human being.

He also had stories of family mystery and intrigue. "Your great great great great grandfather shot and killed a man over a slave woman who had been taken off his place," he told me. "He got a warrant for the arrest of the man, a Mr. Usry." The Sheriff got together a posse to execute the arrest warrant. "When they rode up to Usry's place, Great Grandpa and Mr. Usry started dog cussing each other. Usry refused to surrender and went on verbally abusing Great Grandpa," he continued.

"I bet he said something about Great Grandpa's Mama," I suggested.

"I don't know, he could have," Uncle Buddy replied. "I guess Great Grandpa figured that the talk was over and when Mr. Usry cocked his pistol, Great Grandpa shot and killed him. The Sheriff said it was self defense." Once I got old enough to get a driver's license, I would often leave after school and drive north to see Uncle Buddy. We talked a month of Sundays. I never tired of his stories.

I was just thinking. In addition to my own son, nephew and nieces, I have cousins who have near grown children and within another thirty or forty years, if the Lord tarries, those children could have grandchildren.

Maybe they will come to me and give me the pleasure of telling them about our family. I'll be Uncle Buddy and they will be wide eyed teenage kids. "When I close my eyes," I will tell them, " I can see my mother or her sisters, my aunts, your great great grandmother." I can hear the sound of their voices, the smell of their shoulders, the touch and sometimes punishment of their hands. And before you ask—yes, they all changed my diapers in a previous century. I'll tell them about "Aunt Lou" and "Great Grampa and Mr. Usry," and many many more. I'll also tell them about the man who told me all about all of them.

I eventually went off to school and I rarely saw Uncle Buddy after that. In the late fall of 1977, he sent word through his cousin, my Grandmother, that he wanted to see me. Uncle Buddy was ill. It was a gray day. I think it was late December. It was cold and the leaves had all fallen from the pecan trees. I went to the old house where he lived. I entered through the back door and went directly to the bedroom where he lay.

"It sure is good to see you," Uncle Buddy said as I entered the room. He looked so weak.

"Sit down," he said as he "patted" the heavy blanket with his hand. I sat on the foot of his bed.

"I brought you a Christmas present," I said. Yes, I am now sure that it was December. I handed him a large print family Bible. He thanked me. We talked.

There had been some problems in the Baptist Church which Uncle Buddy had attended most of his life. The church had split apart. I had heard about it, but I just let him tell me, anyway. It was easier for the "political types" among the family to leave the church, but Uncle Buddy was no big time politician. He was a man to whom heritage, history and family continuity meant everything. Uncle Buddy probably had no fear of death, but if he ever thought that his family line would be "cut off"—that would have killed him. This whole church mess was still tearing at his heart.

He was tired and I thought that he needed to rest more than he needed to talk to me. I told him that I had to go, but that I would come back and see him later, when he was up and around. He reached out his hand and gripped mine. His hand was covered with very large "freckles." My hand was covered with smaller ones. His grip was weak. His hand felt cool. Not cold, but cool.

I got in the car and drove South. I wiped my eyes on the sleeve of my shirt. An era was passing. I didn't like it; but there was nothing I could do about it.

I guess it was two or maybe three weeks later— Uncle Buddy died. His funeral was conducted at the new "split off" church. The church organization was new, the church building was not. It was a typical country funeral.

When we began to leave the service, I observed that there were several photographers and cameramen and reporters outside the church. There was a caravan of three or four cars in front of the church. These cars were surrounded by men wearing black suits and dark sunglasses. "What the devil is going on here?" I asked myself. No sooner had I asked that, when the answer hit me. It had to do with Uncle Buddy's little brother's son. He happened to be the then President of the United States.

That was over 22 years ago. William Alton, "Uncle Buddy" Carter would be 111 years old today. He was more than just some distant kin to me. He was my friend and I still miss him.

A Heart in Need of a Hug

It never ceases to amaze me how God can change the human heart when we are willing to be changed.

I received this letter and I think we all need to hear it:

Dear Mr. Revell,

I was having such a nice day, laying on the beach watching my two children frolic in the surf, listening to Florida Public Radio, when the narrator began to read an article written by you, entitled Muster the Troops—There's Genocide in Bosnia. I was shocked that FPR would read *anything* written by you, but as I listened to your description of the birth of your son, I found myself fighting back tears.

It brought me back to the birth of my own two children, the most wonderful blessing that anyone can receive. But then, you did it. You switched direction on me and my tears of joy turned to stark raving madness. I started screaming at you—hoping you could hear me through the radio. I then took my ice chest and, heaving it up, smashed the radio into the sand. Other beach goers were looking at me and the children came running back to me asking, with concern, "Mommy, are you alright?" I had never done anything like this, and they were; frankly, shocked.

We didn't speak a word on the way home. I just told them that I was very upset with one of the commentators on the radio, but that I had overreacted.

I couldn't tell them the truth, how could I? I have always been in favor of the legality of abortion . . .

although, having now birthed two very much loved children . . . listening to your essay raises questions that I don't really want to consider.

You see, in my teenage years, I had an abortion. It was the most difficult decision I ever had to make. I was sixteen. My "boyfriend" at the time dumped me when he found out. He wouldn't return my calls, and refused to have anything further to do with me—except when I occasionally saw him laughing with his friends in the hallway at school—although, he usually stopped laughing and averted his eyes when I passed by.

My parents were very staunch Baptists and it would have devastated their trust in me as well as their reputation in the community. I was emotionally destroyed. I was attempting to carry on the charade that everything was all right, to my family, friends, and church leaders, but inside, I was dying. Every day, I would have to excuse myself several times from class, or from dinner, to go into the bathroom to cry. I woke up every morning feeling sick to my stomach, and the tears would just flow out for several minutes before I could compose myself enough to get out of bed. I told everyone that I was staying up late to study— to explain my constantly bloodshot eyes, and that I must have a mild case of lingering food poisoning to explain my constant nausea.

I just couldn't face the humiliation that would come with acknowledging my condition. I knew my parents would never, ever, ever forgive me for this. I felt that I just couldn't survive the humiliation. I contemplated suicide over and over. Then, I took the only avenue I thought I had to survive emotionally—abortion.

Since that time, I have been an active participate in the pro-choice movement. I felt that I needed to stand up for others who faced the same hardship as I. Yet all this time I have been haunted by thoughts that I have always pushed to the back of my mind. Thoughts about the child who was, but yet never came to be.

Would she have had blue eyes like mine? Would she have liked chocolate milkshakes and wading in mudpuddles with rubber boots like my kids do now? Would she have been able to bring tears to my eyes just by that first little dimpled smile? Would she have cried when ET "died" in Spielberg's classic, like my kids did? Would I gladly give my life to protect her, as I would for my children?

But yet, I didn't. By your reckoning, I took her life from her, before she even had the opportunity to live it. Mr. Revell, who can live with that? No one. So, you see, how can I accept your position? I can't even think about it.

I can't believe that I am writing you this letter. I don't really know why. I fully intended to vote for Al Gore, but now, I just don't know.

--Donni, in PCB

Dear Donni,

Some years ago there was a man who had done some pretty bad things. After getting a woman who was married to someone else pregnant, this guy then killed the woman's husband in order to cover-up what he had done. That man is a "blood-kin" relative of my wife, and, consequently, my son, Governor Boudreaux. He had a hard time facing what he had done, and when he did—the guilt was overwhelming. He did find peace; I'll let him tell you.

Muster the Troops—There's Genocide In Bosnia

Oh, what joy for those
whose rebellion is forgiven,
whose sin is put out of sight!

Yes, what joy for those
whose record the Lord has cleared of sin,
whose lives are lived in complete honesty!

When I refused to confess my sin,
I was weak and miserable,
and I groaned all day long.
Day and night your hand of discipline
      was heavy on me.
My strength evaporated like water
      in the summer heat.

Finally, I confessed all my sins to you
And stopped trying to hide them.
I said to myself, "I will confess my
      rebellion to the Lord."
And you forgave me! All my guilt is gone.

Therefore, let all the godly confess their
      rebellion to you while there is time,
That they may not drown in the
      floodwaters of judgment.
For you are my hiding place;
You protect me from trouble.
You surround me with songs of victory.

The Lord says, "I will guide you along
      the best pathway for your life.
I will advise you and watch over you.
Do not be like a senseless horse or mule
That needs a bit and bridle to keep it under control

Many sorrows come to the wicked,
But unfailing love surrounds those
who trust the Lord.
So rejoice in the Lord and be glad,
all you who obey him!
Shout for joy, all you whose hearts are pure!

--King David, Psalm 32.

Donni; I hope it's ok, if I call you that. Do me a favor and wrap your arms around yourself. Now gently squeeze. Thanks, I needed that—maybe we both did.

I think you are going to make a wonderful advocate for the inherent value of human life as well as the pro-choice of sexual abstinence. What if this informed "you" had been there for the teenage "you"? Maybe the heartache could have been avoided. That, Donni, is something worth fighting for.

That Place has Caught Fire

It is interesting how "religion" often thwarts the very things that God, himself, seeks to do with us . . . While adults have a hard time with this concept, children seem to easily grasp it . . . But then again, the Bible does say "unless you change and become like little children, you will never enter the kingdom of heaven" . . .

I grew up as most children in the South of that day, recognizing that there were basically two different kinds of people; at least within the context of religion. You were either a sprinkler or a dunker. We were sprinklers. In our church, the preacher wore a black robe, sort of like a judge. The people, at least the ones who weren't snoring, sat very quiet and very still, kind of like you would at a funeral. There were only two acceptable movements during the service. One was an occasional elbow from an embarrassed wife, as she jabbed a snoring husband in the ribs. The other was the constant fanning of ones' self with a church bulletin or with a small cardboard picture of the church stapled to a wooden paint stir stick.

I observed that our pastor's sermons would always fall into one of two categories. The first were the "factoids," which dealt principally with the children of Israel. There also was a lot of begetting in that category. The old testament was largely taught as a history lesson. Secondly there was New Testament, limited, very limited, social commentary. These were the days of the civil rights movement and the slightest suggestion of interracial unity would be met with great disdain. The old men would grumble after the service, "He's done stopped preaching and gone to meddling." A meddling preacher was an unemployed preacher.

During the summers, I would have my religious and work horizons expanded. Once school let out, me and Grandpa Bennett would farm six days a week. Depending upon the year, "we" would grow cotton or corn or milo and of course, white faced beef cattle. The other day belonged to the Lord, and except for Grandma Bennett fixing our meals on that day; we didn't so much as hit a lick at a snake. We often spent those afternoons sitting on the front porch talking. Everything was quiet on those Sundays. Not a tractor in the county moved on that day.

I never heard a "faith" based disagreement between Grandpa and Grandma Bennett. I'm sure that there must have been some, but they had obviously worked that out many years before. Grandma Bennett attended a very traditional Dunker church in a very traditional brick building with a paved parking lot and landscaping and a pipe organ.

Grandpa Bennett attended a different church. It was an old wooden structure that hadn't seen a coat of paint since Roosevelt . . . that would be Teddy. The cars, mostly farm trucks, were parked in the sand under the big oaks, and the only landscaping around the place had been put there by God, himself. I may be beating a dead horse at this point but; they didn't have a pipe organ.

Most Sundays I would go to church with Grandma Bennett. Her church was very much like our sprinkler church. There were some differences. The preacher didn't wear a robe, which made him look very much like all the regular men. He got excited when he preached and even slapped the Bible a couple of times. Our "sprinkler" pastor never got excited and he certainly never slapped the Bible. This man's face would turn blood red and he sweated like a hog as he warned against the fires of hell. I had never seen our pastor sweat, and the only times he ever mentioned hell was to the capacity crowds that appeared on Easter Sunday or on the Sunday that fell closest to Christmas. I imagine he figured that there was no reason to warn the faithful regulars as he would just be "preaching to the choir." They had a dunking pool. We had a small bottle of water from The Jordan river. It rested on a red velvet cushion in the sanctuary. Grandpa Bennett's church had a creek or a river or a pond. I suppose that made them dunkers too, but that's where the similarity ended.

I never went to a dunker church in my life where a fight didn't break out, right in the middle of the sermon. The fights were verbal disagreements and never came to blows. As the preacher sweated, slapped his Bible and pounded on the pulpit, one group would yell for him to keep going; "Preach it brother!" they would scream. The second group would yell for the preacher to bring it to an end so everyone could go home and eat. That group would scream, "Amen." "Amen," as I well knew, was Bible language for "the end." That's why they put it at the end of every hymn and every prayer. The one group, I figured, had eaten a bigger breakfast than the other.

We once had a woman in our sprinkler church who married a dunker. We were all sitting there as usual, being quiet and very still. There was only the distant hum of someone snoring and the voice of the pastor. "For the scripture sayeth, whosoever believeth on him shall not be ashamed. For there is no difference between the Jew and the Greek; for the same Lord over all is rich unto all that call upon him."

"God talks a lot like Shakespeare," I thought, as I struggled to keep my eyes open.

"For whosoever shall call upon the name of the Lord shall be saved," the pastor concluded.

"Preach it brother!" the dunker yelled from the back row. Everyone in the place awakened immediately and all three hundred or so pairs of eyes turned and focused dead on him. His new bride "slunk" down into the pew, more embarrassed than she had ever been in her entire life. The next week she came to church alone. They were getting something called a divorce. A divorce was where you couldn't live in the same house together or talk face to face ever again. A little old lady wearing a hat with flowers on it took her hand and "patted" it saying, "It's ok darling, mixed marriages are so hard to hold together."

This particular Sunday, I was going to church with Grandpa Bennett. I had never been to church with him before. "Now this church is a little different than what you're used to," he warned.

"A little different? How?"

"It's just a little different—you'll see."

I was thinking about what could possibly be different. How could it be different? In what way could it be different? Then it hit me.

"Grandpa—they don't hold snakes in your church do they?"

"Not generally."

I sat there in fear. Not generally . . . What does that mean? I thought. It means that sometimes they do, and what if this was snake day . . . I ain't going in if it's snake day. Grandpa Bennett would divorce me for sure, but I ain't going into a church with a bunch of snakes. He must have seen the terror in my eyes, because he reached over with that huge "farmer worn" hand, rubbed the top of my head and said, "Son, there are no snakes in the church." Whew! I breathed a deep sigh of relief! If it ain't snakes, what is it that's different? I returned to my original thought.

About that time we pulled the big truck up into the front yard of the church, I hopped out and was paralyzed dead in my tracks by the screaming and the "hollering" coming from the open church doors. "You said they didn't have snakes," I protested. "There are no snakes in there," Grandpa insisted.

Although I didn't see any smoke, I said, "Grandpa, I think the place has caught fire."

"Come on son."

"But Grandpa?"

"Come on."

I ran up close to his leg and you couldn't have slipped a sheet of Blue Horse notebook paper between us for the next two hours. These people lifted their hands up toward heaven. Some shouted praises. Some danced. Some laughed and some cried tears of joy. The preacher was more "dunker" like in his delivery. He talked about King David stripping down to his fruit of the looms and dancing with all of his might before the Lord. God declared David to be a man after His own heart. It seems that David's wife had watched his dancing and wasn't the least bit impressed. She told David that a king shouldn't act like a fool, and that she was embarrassed by his behavior.

After the service, me and Grandpa Bennett headed back home. I thought about the experience. He hummed "Amazing Grace."

"Grandpa," I said. "Do you suppose that King David and his wife got a divorce?"

"No. I wouldn't think so."

"Grandpa, I don't reckon King David could come to our church, but I imagine his wife would feel right at home. I expect he would have to go to your church."

"He'd be welcome, too," Grandpa Bennett added.

Yeah, I figured he would be.

V

Hillary, Queen of Denile

Hillary and the Truman Show

Hillary Rodham Clinton, candidate for the U.S. Senate has come to the tiny Florida village of Seaside for a $10,000 per plate fundraising dinner for her New York campaign. This village is the set for the motion picture "The Truman Show" starring Jim Carey. The premise is that a child is orphaned in infancy and adopted by a mega-corporation which produces "The Truman Show," a 24 hour a day, 30 year running television program which features the daily life of Truman (Carey).

The world tunes in and watches the program fully aware that it is merely a show. Truman lives in a virtual world in which everything is staged, created and phony. Even the sunrise, sunset, moon and rain are fake. Although the rest of the world sees that Truman's world is not real, he knows nothing of the "real" world. He only knows the fake and phony world in which he lives. That world is "reality" to him. He knows of no other.

As Hillary's six car entourage entered the village, a young man looking remarkably like Jim Carey called out, "Welcome home Hillary, I've been expecting you."

Hillary May Not Bake Cookies . . . But She Belly Dances for Votes

U.S. Senate candidate Hillary Rodham Clinton and her rolling dog and pony show have belly danced once again for Arab extremists.

This time the fundraiser was in Massachusetts and the American Muslim Alliance coughed up 50,000 big ones. This group demands that Israel surrender the land that God himself gave them and that they turn it over to the Palestinians, including the city of Jerusalem. The same city where King David danced in his underwear thousands of years before there even was such a thing as a Muslim, or a Christian for that matter. Although, if you read David's 32nd Psalm, that last one is debatable anyway.

It was reminiscent of Hillary's 1998 call that Israel give up part of its country to create a separate nation for the Palestinians. They would no doubt establish a terrorist training camp there to maim and kill the Israeli citizens. Mrs. Miss. Ms. Clinton, Rodham Clinton, Rodham (whatever) says that she is returning every penny of the $50,000. "I didn't know it was a Buddist, uh . . . a Muslim Temple," she responded. Clinton's opponent Rick Lazio called the payoff, that is the donation, "blood money."

Perhaps Uncle Jean-Thomas said it best: "gettin' Hillary to cough back up dat money is like gettin' a Cajun to give up crawfish—even for lent."

I was just thinking . . .

Maybe we could make Fidel an even swap—New York City for Cuba. Cuba is a beautiful place and New York is a lot further from Florida than Cuba. Besides,

Castro would probably have his hands full with terrorist bombings in the Bronx or across the river in Newark to even bother to think about fooling with us down here. I was once in Newark and I can't see what real difference another bomb or two would make to the place.

Oh well . . . . . Can't a man dream?

VI

Ruminations of a PhobaPhobic Zoophile

It's About Time I Confess, I'm a "Phobaphobe"

The "speech police" and the "thought police" have, in recent years sought to keep the rest of us under control by systematically changing our language, or by creating new words to describe their liberal disgust for traditional American values. Sometimes they will simply change the definition of the word, itself; such as the word "gay."

When I was a child, we sang an old song left over from the War for Southern Independence: I can still remember the words:

When Johnny comes marching home again,
Hurrah! Hurrah!
We'll give him a hearty welcome then
Hurrah! Hurrah!
The men will cheer and the boys will shout
The ladies they will all turn out
And we'll all feel gay,
When Johnny comes marching home.

The old church bell will peal with joy
Hurrah! Hurrah!
To welcome home our darling boy
 Hurrah! Hurrah!
The village lads and lassies say
With roses they will strew the way,
And we'll all feel gay

When Johnny comes marching home.

Get ready for the Jubilee,
Hurrah! Hurrah!
We'll give the hero three times three,
Hurrah! Hurrah!
The laurel wreath is ready now
To place upon his loyal brow
And we'll all feel gay
When Johnny comes marching home.

It's sad, no one sings that song anymore, but then, it seems, no one really feels gay anymore.

The efforts of the Speech Police have produced a barrage of "phobias" that have become a blight on our culture.

Don't get me wrong, I do know that there are actual "phobias," from which many people suffer. There is of course acrophobia; the fear of heights.

Since the movie "arachnophobia" was released, virtually everyone in the country now knows that arachnophobia is the fear of spiders. There are many other lesser known phobias, and here are a few of them (no kidding, this is legit):

Agraphobia – the fear of being sexually abused. (I would assume by the name—by a farm animal)

Agrizophobia – the fear of wild animals. (My guess would be grizzly bears, but since we only have the small black bear in Florida, this phobia is probably quite limited here.)

Arachibutyrophobia—the fear of peanut butter sticking to the roof of your mouth. This phobia mostly plagues small children.

There are many "phobias" which afflict only a particular segment of our society. Some of them even afflict the U.S. Department of Speech Police and its various divisions, such as;

Allodaxaphobia – the fear of opinions (I don't think I need to comment about that one).

Audrophobia – this phobia produces great anxiety among the feminine terrorist section of the USDSP; it is, the fear of men.

Carnophobia – The fear of meat (See column – I Love Cats – they taste a lot like chicken).

Hagiophobia – the fear of things holy; like the family. The U.S. Department of Speech Police, Division of Homosexuals, is particularly susceptible to this one.

Bibliophobia – the fear of the "Book," from which Judeo-Christian culture is derived. That one really leaves them red faced and gasping for air.

There are other "phobias" that have recently attacked Albert, Billy Bob Daley, and the rest of the Gore Campaign. They are:

Arithmephobia – the fear that Billy Bob Daley won't be able to "dig up" the number of votes to highjack the election.

Dikephobia – No it's not the fear of "dikes" you idiot; it's the fear of justice, from the word "diktat," noun; from the Latin word "dictatum." It means, unilaterally imposed settlement that deals harshly with a defeated party.

The Gore Campaign is currently paralyzed with dikephobia. They are terrified that even after the campaign anthropologist Billy Bob Daley "digs" up the "dimples" to "win," with the full blessing of Little Chuckie Wells and the Florida Supremes; the U.S. Supreme Court will dispense justice, and do so harshly.

I hope so; Lord, I reluctantly hope so.

There are also the "phobias" of;

Claustrophobia [pronounced clostra-phobia].

It's the fear of being in an enclosed confined area; like a closet.

Homophobia – anxiety caused by militant homosexuals who came out of the closet. What were they all doing in that closet anyway? Never mind, I don't think I really want to know.

I must admit that I, even I, suffer from the anxiety of phobias, like the dreaded;

Automatonaphobia – the fear of ventriloquist's dummies. (See; Little Chuckie Wells and the Florida Supremes)

And then there is the horrid;

Autodysomophobia – the fear of someone with a putrid or vile odor.

I started to write a list, but this ain't the Sunday New York Times.

Ok. Hillary, Albert, Bill (Clinton & Daley). Don't get me started here. Ted Kennedy. Stop. (At least Teddy did take a bath in the Chappaquidick).

Ok, that's enough.

Oh, I almost forgot. I'm also;

Phobophobic – all these phobias cause me a great deal of anxiety.

I Love Cats...
They Taste Just Like Chicken

I Love animals. I have many of them: chickens, turkeys, guineas, pigeons, ducks, dogs, parrots, goats, horses, peacocks and more. Animals are fine things . . . some of them taste good too.

"Oh, you're going to catch Hell for that one," my boyhood friend Jim Beau Pendarvis warned.

"What?" I asked

"The PETA people, you know, People for the Ethical Treatment of Animals."

"Oh!" I replied. It seems a bunch of them drove up from Miami and laid siege to the Jackson County Cattle Auction. One of them threw some blood that splattered all over Jim Beau's brand new rattlesnake skin boots, which then caused Jim Beau to get blood and even a couple of boogers all over the knuckles of his right hand.

"Well, those left winger vegetarians couldn't possibly condemn me to Hell, since they don't even believe there is a Heaven or a Hell. So, how could they condemn me to a place they don't even believe exists?" I felt relieved. But then, the Spirit convicted me of feeling relief from their disbelief, so I decided to call them and minister to them.

"People for the ethical treatment of animals," the lady (sorry) the woman, answered the telephone.

"I would like to know why you folks don't believe in heaven or in hell?" I asked.

"Is this a joke?" she responded, just before she hung up the phone.

Having the patience of Job, and recognizing my clear Christian duty, I called back.

"People for the Ethical Treatment of Animals . . ." the lady . . . woman, answered the telephone again.

"I'm considering a sizable contribution to your organization," I responded ". . . and I just have a couple of questions first."

"I'll certainly try to help you if I can," she said.

"Do you people believe in a Heaven and/or Hell?" I asked.

"I'm not sure that PETA has an official position on such things," the woman responded.

"Well, what about you, just you?" I pressed on.

"I'm not certain," she answered diplomatically. "What about you, do you think there are animals in Heaven?" she asked.

"Well of course I do. We know that Jesus has a horse, so I don't see why the rest of us can't have some animals too," I responded. "You see," and I went straight to the point, "We all have fallen short of God's perfect will for our lives . . . " I continued, "that is . . . we are stubborn, sort of like jackasses, and we have all rebelled against God's ways and have chosen to pursue our own ways. His ways are better. If we will give up our jackass ways and follow His ways, He is faithful to forgive us," I said.

"So do you believe that your animals are going to this heaven with you?" she asked.

"Yes, I most certainly do!" I responded. "Well, at least the ones that I've not yet eaten when the time comes," I added.

"Go to Hell, you carniverous *?#=&!" she screamed just before the "SLAM" of the phone.

Another believer. Maybe I should become a preacher.

You Don't Sound "Gay" to Me

It has become very clear to me that many times the words that I put to paper stir a variety of emotions in some readers. I recently received a letter from one of them. At first, I thought the letter was a hoax. I took it to someone I knew in the antique business—someone I knew to be a homosexual. He said it was no hoax, and that, although he disagreed with the letter, the feelings expressed are not uncommon among homosexuals. With that "expert opinion"; here it is:

My dearest Mr. Revell,

I want to inform you exactly what I think of your right wing, christian coalition, moral majority, bull *$#%&. First, I hate Jessie Helms. I also hate Ronald Reagan. I hate Ryan White for making us look like a bunch of disease ridden animals inflicting death on children. I hate the f#*&!% Pope John Paul II and I hate the whole f#*&!% Catholic church. That's right I even hated Mother Teresa. What the hell did she ever do for us? I hate Jerry Falwell. I hate the sanctimonious, self-righteous, Baptist Church too. I hate the police and the military. I hate the Congress and their refusal to recognize our rights. I hate the f#*&!% Supreme Court. I hate William f#*&!% Buckley, Pat Buchanon, and every- f#*&!% -one named Bush. They are all responsible for the mass agonizingly slow deaths of my people over the last 15 years.

I hate straight people who think they are intelligent, witty, or artistic. I hate your stupid little "ideal childhood" stories. I hate that you are allowed to become a father and I am not. Your smug insistence upon the use of the word "homosexual" rather than the commonly accepted term "gay" disgusts me. I am gay. That word belongs to us now and you will never get it back. I hate you.

Sincerely,

The Gay Rooster

If I may respond:

Dear Sir,

There seems to be a lot of hate in you. Hate will eat you like a cancer if you hold on to it. About that word "gay," you don't seem the least bit "gay" to me.

VII

The Big Event . . .
Goes Into Overtime

Jeb, George, Barbara & the General

As the Presidential election comes down to the wire, Floridians are being deluged with recorded telephone messages. So far, Jeb, Barbara, W., and retired General Norman Swartzkoff have all called my house.

George is coming to Fort Walton Beach. I don't know why? He's just preaching to the choir here. George, if you read this, do your son some good and go south old man, go south. There is a strip along the south I-95 corridor. It's a relatively small area, but it has nearly one fourth of the real consistent voters in this state.

Go, let them see your wrinkles. Better yet, take Barbara. Let them know that your son will never abandon the elderly. They need to hear that, and as of this moment they are not hearing it. You'll probably have to "speak up" because, word has it, Al Gore has stolen their hearing aids. I don't know whether you can turn them around at this late date, but it's worth a shot.

Florida does carry 25 electoral votes. Of course, I know that you know that. You could even call Dr. Laura and get her to broadcast her radio program from Boca Raton for this last week. Afterwards she could conduct a march with Jewish Clergy; call it "Rabbis for W."

Well, it couldn't hurt.

Election Day–Florida Central

At the time that I penned these words, I certainly had no idea that my friends and neighbors in tiny precinct 18 at the Santa Rosa Beach Community Church would literally select the next President of the United States. Think about that for a moment—but for the Bush landslide in my own neighborhood—Albert would be implementing his socialist agenda today.

6:00 am Santa Rosa Beach, Florida, November 7, 2000.

Change the "Governor Boudreaux's" diaper; now that'll wake you up better than a capuccino. Put the "Governor" in his swing-o-matic and turn on his Willie Nelson compact disc. He loves the red headed stranger's renditions of; Always on my Mind, Without a Song, Georgia on My Mind, Stardust, Danny Boy, Let it be Me, Mona Lisa, Blue Skies, Blue Eyes Crying in the Rain, Wind Beneath My Wings and Over the Rainbow. About half way through the disc he is asleep and I can write today's column.

The Presidential election today will be a squeaker. In Florida, it's going to be tighter than a tick on a dog's . . . well, its gonna be close. Anyone who's been watching this election must have come to the conclusion that Bush and Gore both think Florida's 25 electoral votes and perhaps the whole enchilada are going to be decided in the three county I-95 south corridor; Dade, Broward and Palm Beach counties. This may be so, but surely that ain't the whole ball of wax. There are several smaller states that remain "iffy."

Despite what the press claims, I do not believe that Tennessee, Arkansas and Maine are among them. They will all go to Bush. First, Gore's home state, Tennessee, and Clinton's home state, Arkansas are thoroughly reviled by them. Clinton will never go back to Arkansas; after all, they are disbarring him from the practice of law there. They seem to know what the definition of the word is, is. He'll probably try to talk Hillary into letting him move into her house in New York. What's one more rat in New York anyway? Maine. The Bush's have a summer house at Kennebunkport and I think W. is the only candidate that even knows Maine is a state. Of course, these states carry few electoral votes. A combined 21 votes. Florida alone has 25.

7:15 a.m. I'm going to break here and go cast my own ballot.

7:40 a.m. It was wonderful, I hope you were there to witness it. The Santa Rosa Beach Community Church Fellowship Hall lent itself today as a polling station. It was a place buzzing with excitement. There were old people, young people, and people in the middle. There were t-shirts identifying some as landscapers and another as a well driller. There was a Sheriff's deputy voting. Realtors, local business owners, and even one lawyer that I knew quite well. "Doing our civic duty," that's how one of my neighbors described it.

It was uniquely American. Not the mere act of voting—They do that around the world. People of diverse backgrounds, occupations, social standing and wealth; all came together here today. Not all thinking alike, but all cooperating in a system set by law. Everyone seemed more than willing to respect the rules, whether their candidate ultimately prevailed or not. There are no armed soldiers here. The only soldiers who enter this place today will do so as citizens and not as an armed militia sent to secure the power of the existing administration. God; what a privilege it is to live in this country. I can't help but note; it was election day two years ago when I last saw my mother alive. She called the evening before to remind me to vote. I did. She was working the polls that day at our local precinct. She died November 10, 1998, and I sure do miss her.

Election Day Eve—
Florida is Indeed Central

5:30 p.m. Central Standard Time, De Funiak Springs, Florida, November 7, 2000.

My brother and I have just signed a contract to sell the home around which many of our childhood memories are based. Well, life goes on. He's headed back to Pace and I'm driving on Hwy 331 south toward Freeport. I just cannot stand having no access to what's going on in this election. I know I'll be home in 25 minutes, but patience is a virtue that I'm still praying for. Ok. For which I am still praying. How many times do I have to do this before you understand that I do know how to "talk right." I hope it (patience) doesn't come to me by tribulation. I spilled coffee on the dashboard of my truck and the coffee ran down into the radio and shorted it out. I'm incommunicado!

My cell phone! I have a cell phone! By now, I'm sure that the media is already projecting east coast returns based on exit polls. It's 6:30 eastern time. I'll call my wife.

"Hello?"

"Have you heard how the election is going?"

"No. I'm feeding the Governor."

133

Great, that's the last time I ever marry a lawyer from Berkeley. I tell you that right now. Where is your activism, woman?

"I'll check, when I get finished feeding the Governor."

"Good heavens."

My cousin Keith, I'll call him. #850-230-XXXX.

"Hello"

"Nicole?"

"Yes, Uncle Ken."

"Let me speak to your dad."

"Well, I'm on the phone with one of my friends, could he call you back in a few minutes?"

Teenagers! As Charlie Brown used to say "Good Grief!"

6:00 p.m. C.S.T. – I'm home frantically searching for election returns. Our parrot, "Birkenstock" (ask my wife) chewed the end off of the satellite remote, so I don't have any television coverage. Ok. Actually, he chewed it up last fall, but I didn't really see any reason to get it fixed. We don't watch much T.V. anyway. Come to think of it; we don't watch any television at all—at least not since last fall.

Talk Radio—they'll be covering the election returns. Whew, I found it. "And we are announcing Florida and Michigan have gone to Gore."

What! What!

That's it, it's over.

What about Pennsylvania?—that's the last possible hope. "Pennsylvania goes Gore."

Damn!

"Honey, what is your parents' telephone number.

"(510) 524-XXXX"

I still can't believe he's taken Florida. The polls here in the panhandle are still open for 45 more minutes. This is bull. What are the numbers. How close is it. That announcement will keep people from voting here, and we know Bush will carry northwest Florida, two to one. That announcement could produce its own result. People here are just getting home from work. They are feeding the kids and preparing to go and vote at their neighborhood precinct. That announcement, if it's wrong, just cost Bush ten or fifteen thousand votes. Either way, I guess it's over. Fine.

"Gore wins!" (But it's a lousy way to win.)

"Honey, what is the telephone number for your parents?"

"I told you; 510-524-XXXX."

"Hello."

"Well it's over; it's a done deal."

"What?"

"They announced Pennsylvania and Florida both for Gore.

"Maybe they're wrong. How do they know?"

"Exit poles are pretty accurate; they know."

"Your part of Florida is completely for Bush."

"I know, but the media's announcement of Gore as the winner, while our polls are still open will quash at least ten or fifteen thousand votes here."

"Well, don't be so excited, it may not be over."

"Yeah, right!"

Ok; the South I-95 corridor has indeed elected the President of the United States of America. I hope you look into the eyes of your grandchildren tomorrow and tell them the truth; "I voted to make sure that you don't have it better than me."

W. Wins ... or Does He?

November 8, 2000. I'm not sure of the exact time, as the "Governor Boudreaux" didn't sleep well last night. I think he was concerned about the voucher issue. I have learned in a mere month of being a father; if your baby don't sleep—you don't either. Other than a swing-o-matic, a bassinet, a bouncie seat and numerous other baby paraphernalia strewn about the place—I think I'm at home; so I'll add to the log date above—Santa Rosa Beach, Florida.

Does anyone in America truthfully know just what happened last night?

First Gore—then Bush—then Nobody.

It seems that all of the networks called Florida for Gore even before the northwest Florida precincts, including ours, had closed. I hate that. In some races it doesn't seem to matter, but in this one, it could be the difference in who becomes the next President of the United States and for all practical purposes; the leader of the free world. Now it matters.

At about 1:40 a.m. this morning, V.P. Al Gore telephoned George W. Bush to concede the presidential election. W. thanked him for the call. It's a tradition in America. We don't go to war, we just accept the lawful outcome of an election. Sometimes we even accept it as in 1960 when Richard Daley's graveyard votes elected JFK President.

Well, it's our system, nobody said it was perfect. At least we don't go to war over it. At least not yet.

But wait. At about 2:00 o'clock this morning, Gore called W. back again.

GORE: I take it back, I ain't conceding.

BUSH: Do what?

GORE: I ain't conceding Florida or the election.

BUSH: You cain't take it back.

GORE: I just did. Richard, ah, that is Bill Daley told me that Florida is too close to call.

BUSH: Tell that fat ass Daley to go back to counting graveyard votes in Chicago. We don't need no trash like him down here. Besides, my baby brother swears that I got you whipped in Florida. Votes are still coming in from the Panhandle and I could beat the snot out of you in that part of the state with both hands tied behind my back.

GORE: Your baby brother ain't callin' this dance, Monsieur.

BUSH: If I could reach through this phone, we'd settle this thing right now. I've been wanting to whip your wimpy nerd butt ever since I first saw you. You remind me of Clarence Bates, a nerd in the third grade. You couldn't miss the urinal without Clarence calling the law.

GORE: Well, you don't have to get snippy.

BUSH: Snippy? Snippy? Did you say snippy?

GORE: Yes. Snippy.

BUSH: Figures, Clarence Bates loved that word. He even named his pet mouse Snippy. Do you have a pet mouse, Albert?

GORE: I ain't talking to you anymore, and don't call me Albert.

RU 1784 – The Day After Vote

7:00 pm, November 8, 2000, Santa Rosa Beach. W. wins by 1,784 votes, but stop the presses. I told you that this would be a squeaker. I never dreamed it would be this close. State law requires, in instances in which the margin of victory is one half of one percent or less, that we recount the votes. Fine, run 'em through again boys, but do it fast.

Gore has dispatched William Daley to the south I-95 corridor to "dig up a few votes." I'm not sure what they intend on doing at this late date, but then I don't have the criminal mind that they do. If you think they are flying here just to watch the machines re-declare W. the winner, you're nuts. That ain't the Daley family tradition. Remember, we still have the absentee military ballots to count and they will run 65-70% Bush, and Daley and the Gore people know it.

Word has it that some organization, I can't imagine who that would be, started calling elderly voters in Palm Beach County last night to let them know that they probably voted for Buchanon instead of Gore. The streets are now filled with old people demanding the head of Theresa Lepore, their elected supervisor of elections, a Democrat.

The Gore campaign has even rented a riot from Jesse Jackson. The Jackson people are expected to riot tomorrow. I hope that no one in the media shows up.

That brings up another thing. The butterfly ballot that Jackson and Daley are squawking about; that ballot is used in Chicago—Cook County Illinois. That's where they are both from, and where they both should go back to as quickly as possible. Let them start a riot in Chicago claiming that Jesse Jackson, Jr. got elected to Congress from a Chicago district only because the voters were confused by the ballot.

Mark my words, Al Gore will be harder to run out of office than Slobodan Milosevic, no matter what the recount reveals.

VIII

OK, It's Double Overtime

The Day After
The Day After Vote

I suppose that it has become obvious to us all why Al Gore dispatched William Daley to our lovely and previously peaceful state, yesterday. His presence has absolutely nothing to do with observing the recount of votes here. Make no mistake about it, he is here to stir up whatever stink he can find and if he can't find any, he'll make some. These people have no conscience and their personal ambition and lust for power supercedes any concern for anyone else or for the well-being of our nation.

There is an element of heartless cruelty to the Democrats calling elderly Jews on election day eve telling them that they may have voted for Buchanon by mistake. In case you didn't know, Buchanon don't much like Jews. Many of these people wear numbers from Auschwitz and other like places on the memory of their minds. They can still see the numbers tattooed on their parents or grandparents. A few need only look at their own wrists. Frightening the elderly people with lies about a planned Republican destruction of Social Security or Medicare is one thing; that's merely despicable. What they are doing in Palm Beach County is a new low for a presidential campaign. I don't know that Bill Clinton himself could top this one. I ask you, what is the problem with the butterfly ballot?

    a. the ballot was created by an elected Democrat supervisor of elections.

    b. The candidates' names were printed in very large type to be easily read by the elderly.

c. Arrows lead from the name of the candidate directly to the hole to be punched.
d. Gore didn't win.

Sally Mae Forehand
Demands a Recount

The runner up to the 1976 Queen of the Annual Collard Festival in Hosford is demanding a recount. She has asked Lester Noles, the notary public at the laundry mat to assist her in the effort. Lester, a local organizer of the 1979 Tractorcade to Washington, D.C. has some pretty slick plans on overturning the vote.

First of all, "Sally Mae has called the lovely Brandi Glasscock and officially retracted her concession," says Noles. In order that there be no doubt about this, Lester played an audio tape of the telephone conversation between Sally Mae and the lovely Brandi.

Ring-a-ding-Ring-a-ding-Ring-a-ding.

GLASSCOCK: Good morning, Glasscock residence, Brandi speaking.

FOREHAND: This here's Sally Mae Forehand and I take back my concession and hereby reclaim my crown.

GLASSCOCK: Who is this?

FOREHAND: Sally Mae Forehand.

GLASSCOCK: Who?

FOREHAND: I was illegally and improperly denied my right to the crown as the 1976 Collard Festival Queen.

GLASSCOCK: Oh. I remember you now, you were the fat one. Sally Mae, you should have entered the sow competition at the Liberty County Fair. You would have won hands down.

FOREHAND: Shut-up, you hair flitting anorexic little snot. I demand a recount.

GLASSCOCK: All three voting members of the selection team are dead and buried. You can't have a recount.

FOREHAND: Lester, down at the laundry mat; he knows a garbage collector who picks up the trash at the house of a man who bought a book written by Hillary Clinton's spiritualist. You know, the one that conjured up Eleanor Roosevelt so Hillary could get some advice. The man threw the book in the trash, where the garbage collector found it, and now I have it. Me, Lester and the garbageman are going to meet at the graveyard tonight and get an official recount of the votes. You can come if you want to.

GLASSCOCK: Are you insane?

FOREHAND: We could avoid this whole nasty mess if you would just cough up my crown, little miss priss.

GLASSCOCK: When Hell freezes over Sally Mae When Hell freezes over.

"CLICK"

Politics sure has gotten ugly, hasn't it?

It's Florida State – Again!

We have finally gotten a break from the presidential broo-ha-ha and today we get to watch the legitimate battle in Florida. Number 3 ranked Florida State versus Number 4 ranked Florida. They each came into this game as possible contenders for the National Title. The Seminoles have been the Atlantic Coast Conference Champions eight years in a row and the Gators have been the Southeastern Conference Champions seven times.

There was a bit of pre-game excitement on the field as a group of FSU players shouted across the field at Florida Quarterback Rex Grossman—"Your mama voted for Buchanon." FSU coaches quickly stopped the commotion and the game went forward. When it was all said and done it was FSU topping Florida for the third year in a row. The truth is that the Seminoles feasted on Gatortail today; 30-7.

Speaking of 'gator, I hate that chewy stuff. A friend of mine from Port St. Joe used to hunt gators along the backwater of the Appalachicola river. He claimed "it taste like chicken."

He must have been eating rubber chickens.

After the game, I had the pleasure of interviewing a couple of the winning players. The gators were all crawling back to Gainesville. Oh, the value of a Press Pass.

Snoop Jackson, wide receiver from Havana (That's Hayvanna) thinks the electoral college is part of the Political Science Department at FSU. Thank God that he's majoring in early childhood recreation.

148

Amos Barfield, 286 pound right tackle from Paxton said that he really appreciated the fact that Secretary Christopher and Secretary Baker had come to Florida. "Maybe when they get finished with this election 'bidness' one of the secretaries could go to my American History class and take dictation for me," Barfield pondered.

"What's your major, Amos?"

"Pre-Med. I intend on specializing in laser eye surgery down in Palm Beach County. I hear there's a big need for eye doctors down there."

Smart Kid.

IX

Have We Been Chad?

Do We Finally Have Prince Albert in the Can?

Bill Clinton has instructed the White House staff to cooperate with W's transition team. The CIA is scheduled to begin briefing President-elect Bush. It looks like President Clinton has given Gore "the ol' Lewinsky cigar."

Meanwhile, Prince Albert and his merry men continue to march through the swamps of south Florida, from courthouse to courthouse, filing lawsuits against anything that moves. Gore's most recent victim is the famed actor Wally Gator.

In the suit, Gore accuses Wally, a Bush supporter, of escaping from the zoo for the express purpose of

(a) terrorizing elderly Gore supporters at a polling station in Palm Beach County, thereby causing them to become distraught, shake uncontrollably and mispunch the ballot, and

(b) Causing zookeeper, Mr. Twiddle, a well known, uptight, Gore supporter, to miss the election entirely, while he performed his lawful duties searching for Wally.

Gore is requesting that the court declare that all ballots in that particular precinct were actually cast for him, and that Wally be skinned alive and turned into a suitcase. The Gore team published Wally Gator's theme song as evidence of the mis-dead;

Wally Gator
is a swingin' navigator
in the swamp!

153

He's the greatest percolator
When he really starts to romp.

There has never been a greater
Operator in the swamp!
Se ya later, Wally Gater

Gore attorney, David Boies, points out that Wally's own theme song clearly identifies him as an "operator" in "quote—the swamp."

"I believe the court can take judicial notice of the fact that the biggest swamp in the entire state is the Everglades," says Boies.

"And where is the Everglades?" Boies asks, "Directly abutting . . . (he pauses for effect) . . . Palm . . . Beach . . . County!"

We got you now Wally. And Boies asks the court to consider one question.

"How many other Gore ballots are hidden under that stupid little hat that Wally wears?"

Boies has requested that Little Chuckie Wells and the Florida Supremes issue an order that includes a finding of fact that, hidden under Wally's hat, is (whatever the number may be) one vote more than Gore needs to win the election.

Bush attorney, Barry Richard responded, "what the hell kind of a ruling would that be? Did I catch the wrong flight? This ain't Haiti, is it?"

What's next? Word has it that the Gore campaign is looking into a report that Magilla the Gorilla refused, on the very morning of the election, to eat peanuts offered to him from an elderly Broward County woman. The woman was so distraught, according to Gore attorneys, that she went home and drank a fifth of Canadian Mist, and slept through the entire election. But for the willful, intentional and malicious acts of one, Magilla Gorilla, Albert Gore Jr., would have received one additional vote. And the vote of every American—unless that American is in the military—should be counted, or so he claims in the first draft of the lawsuit.

"That all sounds well and good," concedes Gore's main-most crook, Bill Daley. "But what if the Sho 'Nuff Supremes muzzle 'OUR', that is, the Florida Supremes?" Daley asks, "what then? Where do you have to go around here to buy a decent judge anyway? This ain't like Chicago."

"Why did we ever impeach Alcee Hastings? Alcee wasn't cheap, but at least he could be bought. Judges are like cops, there's never a crooked one around when you need one."

GORE: Shut up with the excuses, Bill. We've got a crisis here, in case you haven't noticed.

DALEY: No; you shut up you stinking little nerd. If it wasn't for me there wouldn't even be a crisis; your nerd ass would be standing on some tree stump in Tennessee trying to explain to a gopher why you lost. . . . I don't wanna hear it—Albert. How long are you planning on fighting this thing—until hell freezes over?

GORE: Until the earth burns-up, Bill. Don't you know global warming is occurring? Didn't you read my book? You said you read my book.

DALEY: As long as you got the money—we got the time. It's not like I got something better to do. I'm sure that I can dig up a few more votes Mr. Vice President.

GORE: That's the old team spirit—Go get 'em boys.

Will this Liberal Court Behave?

Now that Leon County Circuit Court Judge Terry Lewis has ruled that Secretary of State Harris did lawfully exercise her discretion in telling the counties to wrap this thing up and get the vote count into her office, the matter is surely headed to that last bastion of Florida liberalism – The State Supreme Court.

These people do not know the meaning of the words – "judicial restraint." They also don't know the meaning of – "the will of the people." That's how they ignored the fact that 72.8% of "the people" voted for a ballot measure to amend the Florida Constitution, only to have this court strike it down saying the Republican legislature had tricked the voters into approving it.

When Ward Connerly and his group garnered enough signatures to put "colorblind university admissions" on the ballot, the court struck down the wording of all four alternative proposals as "confusing."

In other words, the court prevented the people from voting on whether to eliminate racial consideration in state university admissions. Once again this court saved us from ourselves.

But when this unelected court, and its arm and creation, "The Florida Bar," decided that all Florida judges should enjoy freedom from the people, it began pushing a ballot measure to "educate" voters on the importance of surrendering their right to vote on trial court judges. They published a half million brochures with the slogan, "Vote YES for Qualified Judges, not Politicians." That's right, the judicial branch of the government spent money to sway an election dealing with the future constitutional makeup of the judicial branch of the government.

Some lawyers had a little problem with the scheme so, like any good lawyer would – they filed suit. These lawyers also had a problem with "the litany of falsehoods and half truths . . . " which were being used to educate the voters. It's ok though – The Florida Supreme Court heard the case and ruled that it had done nothing wrong. It helps to be the judge in your own case, don't it? Despite the effort, the poor ignorant masses acting in utter confusion, punched the wrong hole and accidentally kept this right to vote.

How will this unelected-liberal-activist-court decide the election controversy between Liberal Gore and Conservative Bush? Take a guess. Come on folks – This ain't brain surgery.

Little Chuckie Wells & The Florida Supremes

Tallahassee, November 20, 2000.

Five days ago, Florida Secretary of State, Katherine Harris, determined that there was no legitimate reason to continue counting ballots ad infinitum (that means forever) and that she wasn't going to accept any more vote tallies.

Albert, Billy Bob Daley and the Gore legal team went crying back to Leon County Circuit Court Judge Terry Lewis.

GORE: She didn't do what you said!

LEWIS: Yes she did.

GORE: No she didn't. She ain't accepting any more votes.

LEWIS: I never said she had to.

GORE: You did too!

LEWIS: No Albert, I only said that she had to reasonably exercise her discretion. Just because you don't like her decision has nothing to do with it. Now, why don't you boys go play somewhere else.

GORE: We're gonna tell Chuckie Wells and all the other Florida Supremes what you've been doing here, and you'll be in big trouble then. Come on Bill, let's get out of here.

For the first time ever, I felt embarrassed before the world, to be placed in the same "Florida basket of fruit" with the nuts that I observed in Tallahassee today.

I have heard the term Kangaroo Court before, but until today, I could honestly say that I had only once before, personally, witnessed one. That was in the U.S. District Court for the Northern District of Alabama. I have now seen two. There was not even a pretense of justice here today. Perhaps we should be thankful that they didn't just pretend. To call any one of them a "justice" is an affront to the word, itself. "Little Chuckie Wells," the "Chief" among this bunch of "riff-raff," isn't concerned that the entire world is holding its collective breath for a decision. There is no decision to be made. Isn't it obvious that that was done before the hearing today.

The questions posed to the counsel for Secretary of State Harris and counsel for W. were practically militant in content and tone. Sometimes they bordered on the absurd, as when Justice Peggy Quince actually asked this brainstormer;

"Let me ask you, really simply, on a machine—counted ballot, where someone has gone to the polls and they have punched the hole *properly*, but for whatever reason, the chad didn't fall out, are you saying, under your analysis of this—and even if this happened to half the ballots in the county—that there is nothing that can be done?"

Let's check this one out; the chad was "*properly*" punched, but it just refused to fall out. Make your selection;

(a) the chad was being held into place by tiny space aliens hired by the Republican National Committee to thwart the election;

(b) the "chad" itself was a Republican and simply refused to allow a vote for Gore; or

(c) Justice Quince is dumber than a box of rocks.

Governor Chiles appointed Justice Quince to the court on December 8, 1998, a mere four days before he died. He must not have been feeling well that day either. Justice Quince obtained her college degree in Zoology. You think I'm making this up, don't you? Well, I ain't.

It seems to me that Little Chuckie Wells ought to step down and turn the Chief Justice's gavel over to Quince. After all, she has experience as a zookeeper.

These people weren't the least bit concerned about the law as established by the elected representatives of the people of Florida. These "appointed liberal Democrat" justices were only concerned about "fashioning" the outcome by judicial fiat. This is what W. warned about in the presidential debate on October 3rd.

BUSH: "I'll tell you what kind of judges he'll [Gore will] put on there. He'll put liberal, activist judges who will use their bench to subvert the legislature. That's what he'll do."

GORE: "That's not right."

Oh yes it is, Albert. Oh yes it is.

Red Bugs, Moonshine and the Book of Leviticus

*You know something's wrong when your state
Supreme Court decides that the law isn't really
relevant to their legal analysis. I don't understand
nothing—no more! When I was a kid, we walked
five miles to school, in the snow, uphill (both ways)
. . . well, come to think of it, we really don't have
any hills here in Florida and, ok, ok, we don't have
snow either, but it does get pretty darn hot and
humid here, and fighting alligators in the swamp on
the way to school can be a challenge sometimes too.
But my point is this, we were raised to understand
that the law is THE LAW, there's just no getting
around it . . . ; that's just the way it is.*

During the first seven years of my life, I had come
to question nearly everything around me. To some of the
questions, I found adequate answers, but many of them
remained uncompleted puzzles. That is probably because I
couldn't find anyone who really knew the answers.

"You kids stay out of that Spanish moss, there are
red bugs in it!" some adult female in my family called out
to me and my cousins. We had pulled the moss out of a
tree and were wearing it like wigs or holding it to our chins
simulating long gray beards.

We examined the moss carefully and sure enough,
the tiny little red creatures did in fact reside there. "How
do you reck'n she knew there were red bugs in there?" I
asked no one in particular.

162

"She probably had a moss wig sometime and got red bugs in her head," one of my cousins responded, as he began lightly scratching his cranium. Then another began to scratch and as the concept inched its way through each little brain, one by one, we all began to scratch. The scratching became feverish until the youngest broke loose for the porch.

Now that the sissy/cry baby/mama's boy label had already attached to the youngest cousin, who had first run for help, the rest of us were free to seek adult assistance in red bug extermination without fear of social labeling. The whole pack of us ran for the house. My aunt hooked a garden hose through one of the lower limbs of a scrub oak tree and turned the water on full blast. The pump house began to hum as she gave us a couple of bars of soap and supervised our head scrubbing.

When the red bug removal process had been completed to her satisfaction, my aunt turned off the water and instructed us to go around to the front porch and make ourselves "useful."

"Awh!" came a collective sigh from all of the children. We all knew what that meant.

"That's Chinese thumb torture," I thought.

In those days children could not use the word "no," when speaking to an adult member of their own family. If one of us had yelled back, "No! I ain't shelling no butterbeans!" the rest of us would have scattered in order to reduce the likelihood of being injured by the bolt of lightning which would surely strike him dead at any moment.

We had all heard about Clarence Bohannon who had lived in Holmes County. He had actually spoken these forbidden words and schools from all around still took field trips to visit the crater in the Bohannon front yard. There would be no such bolt of lightning here because we all knew better. We reluctantly drug ourselves around the house and onto the front porch. You didn't get struck by lightning for hating butterbean shelling, only for "talking back" or flat refusing to shell them. I knew that one for sure.

I crawled up into the porch swing next to my mother. She pulled the brown grocery sack between us and handed me her bowl, as she went into the house without a word. I knew the routine well. She was going to get me a bowl. Beans in the bowls, hulls in the sack. Beans to the kitchen, hulls to the hogs. Speaking of hogs, I hate hogs. Well, I don't hate them personally, I just hate pork. I don't eat it. I did as a kid because I ate what was prepared and because I couldn't say "no." The closest I ever came to flat refusing to eat what my mother had prepared did involve pork.

"God said this is an unclean meat," I declared from my seat at the table.

"Hush, and eat your pork chops," my mother responded.

I put my fork down on the edge of my plate. All chewing stopped around the table. My mother stared at me as if she were awaiting a further response. My little brother looked across the table at me. His mouth was open and his eyes were as big as moon pies. Sweat began to pop out on his face and I knew what he was thinking. At least I thought I did. But I was on solid ground here. I had God in a catch 22. He couldn't strike me dead with lightning for quoting him, could he? That wouldn't be fair. I may even be able to say that word "no!" and survive. "The whole world as we knew it would be changed," I thought. What if rebellion trumped piety? Where would I be then. I was in a quandary. My mind raced, my mother stared, my brother sweated . . .

Then my brother said, "Kenny, if you say 'it,' can I have your electric train?" My mother laughed. I picked up my fork and ate the pork chops. It just wasn't worth the risk.

When I became grown and obtained the right to full use of the word, I would and still do draw it like a gun. "No! I ain't eatin' no hog!" I finally declared. I don't eat hogs because of what hogs eat—anything and everything. I once saw a hog eat a live snake. Well, it was alive when the hog first started on it. Hogs eat cow doo-doo, their own doo-doo, rotten food with maggots in it and even butterbean hulls.

I had also heard about Thad Larkins. He had gotten into a bad batch of moonshine and went out to slop his hogs; mason jar in one hand, slop bucket in the other. Mr. Larkins passed out right in there with the hogs. When he was finally discovered, two hogs were still eating on what little remained of him as well as eating on another of their own species who had dropped dead next to Mr. Larkins. The dead hog had died from eating the mason jar. Come to think of it, maybe it was the contents of the jar and not the glass that had killed the hog, and maybe Mr. Larkins too. Like I said, hogs will eat anything, and I don't eat things that will eat me. No, I don't eat alligator either. I have eaten it years ago, but I am now armed with the word "No!" I also don't like the texture of alligator, it's "chewy."

"Gator is very good . . . taste like she-cone," a friend tried to convince me.

"I don't know what kind of chicken you've been eatin'," I responded. "Must have been a rubber chicken."

"Mama, why do red bugs live in moss?"

"I suppose they like it there. Shell your butterbeans."

"Moss doesn't have roots. Does moss suck water from the tree?"

"I don't know son. Shell your butterbeans."

"Why is it that only the first one that runs for help is a sissy/cry baby/mama's boy?"

"I don't know son. That really doesn't make much sense does it?"

"Have you ever drank any moonshine like what Mr. Larkins was drinking when his hogs ate him?"

"No! Shell your butterbeans."

"Why . . ."

"Son."

"Yes Mama."

"Give me your bowl and go play somewhere."

Here, in this century, things seem so different. Sometimes I feel out of place here. But, as I stand gazing out of my window, I see children pulling spanish moss out of an oak tree behind my house. They are making wigs and long gray beards out of it. These are the children of those same children who did the same thing some three and a half decades ago.

"Honey!" I called out for my wife who was in the back of the house.

"What is it?"

"Could you bring me two bars of soap."

"Did you say two?"

"Yes, two!"

"Why two?"

166

Have We Been Chad?

"We don't have any butterbeans, do we?
"What?"
"Never mind."

To Be or Not To Be ... A Sissy-Crybaby-Mama's Boy

I actually wrote this column long before the 2000 election fiasco, but it just cries out to be included in this book. This one's for you, Albert.

The Dixie League baseball teams had ended their season. These were the dog days of summer now, where the mercury would top 100 degrees many times before the start of the next school year. The Dixie League teams were made up of boys ages 9-12. The nine and ten year olds rarely got to play, but they were afforded an opportunity to practice and hone their skills with their more advanced teammates. They were also taught that patience and diligence would eventually pay off.

During the season, no kid under nine years of age could so much as touch a grain of dirt or a blade of grass on the playing field unless accompanied by a "real" league player. The penalty for such an infraction would likely be a sock in the eye or a kick right in the stomach from a much older kid. I didn't take to pain very well. I figured that I'd just wait out the season at which time the place would be open to all.

It was the crack of dawn. The sun was not yet blazing. Little boy fists were excitedly pounding on our back door. I opened it, still half asleep. "Grab your glove and come on, we're getting up a game," Jim Beau and Russell and Tommy were all instructing me at the same time.

"Hurry!" one of them said as I slowly walked back to my room to put on my clothes. They all followed me. "Come on, Kenny, kick it into high gear," Jim Beau said.

"You gotta make hay while the sun shines," Russell added.

"For Pete's sake Russell, shut up!" Jim Beau responded.

"I ain't going to shut up—it's a free country!" Just as the eight year old equivalent of a bar brawl was about to break out in my bedroom, my mother stepped into the doorway.

"Boys, boys, boys. It's a little early for this isn't it?" my mother asked.

Was she condoning the behavior and merely objecting to the timing? What if it occurred after cocktail hour? Would this behavior then be acceptable? Are a mother's comments to eight year old boys really responsible for future bar brawls? I wish I had thought to question my mother about this at the time, but like I said, I was still half asleep.

We ran from house to house collecting other boys as we went. Timothy Philpot was the same age as us, but he had an older brother named Mark. Mark was a baseball legend, which brings us to the point of this whole thing. Mark was ten, we were only eight, and he had seen action in the last game of the season. He scored the winning run. The game was tied, but the coach had a winning strategy.

"Philpot!" The coach called to the dugout. "Get up here Philpot! You're on deck!"

Mark looked around as if there were anyone else named Philpot there in the dugout.

"Philpot, I want you to get up there and crowd the plate." The coach lowered his voice, but it was still loud

169

enough for us to hear every word as we clung to the fence.
"Oates will try to brush you back. When he does, lean into
the ball."

"What?" Mark asked as if he had misunderstood.

"You heard me Philpot. Now, get up there and take
it like a man."

Mark trembled as he walked slowly to the plate. He
looked back at the dugout, where the entire team stood
watching him.

"We're counting on you Philpot!" the coach yelled.

Just as he had been instructed, Mark crowded the
plate. The first pitch was low and inside. Mark continued
hugging the plate. The next pitch was a fastball, high and
inside. Way inside. Mark turned just as if he was trying to
avoid the pitch. He didn't. Square in the back. Mark hit
the ground and rolled in agony. The coach ran to his
injured player, as if he were completely surprised at what
had just occurred.

"Philpot, are you ok?" the coach asked as he knelt
down beside him.

"I think so," Mark moaned, trying to hold back the
tears. I could tell he wanted to cry, but his mama isn't here,
so, what would the point be? He had taken the pitch like a
man. Don't ruin it by crying now, I thought.

"Shake it off, Mark!" I yelled from outside the
chain link fencing. "Shake it off' means; "this is a man's
game, don't embarrass yourself and your whole family by
acting like a sissy-crybaby-mama's boy. This was a pivotal
moment in the life of a 10 year old boy. What he did in the
next two minutes would determine how he would be seen
by others for the rest of his life.

Fifty years from now, one of the other players
would run into Mark Philpot on the street. They would

each have their grandsons with them. They would greet each other.

"Afternoon," they would each say. They would introduce their grandsons and talk about the weather. Depending on what Mark Philpot did right now, this minute, would determine the rest of the conversation. If he shakes it off, the old man on the street will tell the two grandsons the story of a boy hero. He will look at Mark's grandson as he tells the story. "Your grandfather," he would say, "once took a 65 or 70 mile an hour fastball right in the back. I know that it must have hurt like the dickens, but he didn't cry, he just shook it off and took his base." Mark would swell with pride as his grandson absorbed the story.

On the other hand, if Mark cried, the conversation on the street would end with no mention of the incident. As they walked away, the old man would tell his grandson how the Mr. Philpot that they were just talking to, had once gotten hit in the back with a baseball and cried like a baby.

"He probably is still a sissy-crybaby-mama's boy," the old man would say.

The old man's grandson would respond, "I expect his grandson is too, paw paw."

"Mark got up," the crowd screamed and applauded him.

His little brother Timothy leaned into me, breathed a sigh of relief, and said, "I thought he'd cry for sure."

"I knew he wouldn't cry," I responded.

"I was just thinking," Timothy shared, "If he'd started squalling, I was going to ask your mother if I could come and live with you. I wouldn't eat much and I could sleep under your bed. I would tell everybody at school that there had been a terrible mix-up in the hospital and that I wasn't really related to him at all."

"Take your base!" the homeplate umpire screamed. Mark took second on a wild pitch, and scored on a double to right field. The crowd went ballistic. I was happy for him. I know his grandson will be proud, too . . . someday.

Chad Who?

Weren't we all happier when "Chad" was just a fairly uncommon male name. I know I was.

Of course, there is also the country of "Chad" in Central North Africa. According to the U.S. State Department, Idriss Deby, the President of Chad was "elected" in 1996 in an election marred by widespread fraud, vote-rigging, and "local irregularities." It sparked an open rebellion in parts of the Country. Sound familiar?

As we all now know, "chad" is the name given to the perforated "flake" of paper that is punched out the back of a voting card. This card can then be fed into a computer and the vote count tallied. Pretty simple? Is anything simple anymore? It's been simple for the last forty years, at least until now.

To complicate matters further; a chad may be "hanging," "swinging," "dimpled," or "pregnant." A chad is referred to as "hanging" when a single corner of the chad is detached or hanging off. A chad is "swinging" if two corners are detached. What if three corners are hanging off? I think that is a "ménage a trois" chad. All of these are counted as votes in a manual recount. Ok. Fine.

The pregnant chad; is, of course, where there is a bulge in the flake of paper, but it is still completely attached. If there is the slightest indentation in the chad, it is referred to as "dimpled."

For the last decade, pregnant chads and dimpled chads *have not* been counted as votes in Florida. But, hold on Mildred, we just got a new set of rules, especially re-designed by the Democratic canvassing boards in the south

173

I-95 corridor. Of course, these rules were only changed when it looked like the manual recount would result in W. winning . . . again. The unmitigated gall!

In fact, I hear that Miami-Dade has, located in South Beach precincts, a "significant number" of voter cards that are being identified as having homosexual chads. There is an indentation but it was "poked" from the rear. The Gore campaign has requested that each of these ballots be counted as two votes. William Daley, the main-most crook in the Gore campaign, has accused the Republicans of attempting to silence the "gay" vote. "Every vote should count," Daley said, "that is, unless it's a military vote."

Hillary Wants to Scrap the College

Senator-elect . . . .
. . . sorry, I had to go and throw up, Hillary Clinton, one
day after her election victory in New York has called for a
"scrapping" of the electoral college. Why? Because it
stands as a hindrance to the election of liberals in a nationwide tally. Hillary wants to change the rules because that's
the only way she could become President.

Some say the electoral college is an outdated form
of electing the President and it ought to go. But, hold the
phone Myrtle, let's take a closer look at it.

The United States is a Republic, not a Democracy.
Put your wig back on and let's talk about it. First of all,
laws are not passed by the popular vote of the people, but
rather are determined by elected representatives. Who are
they? The House and the Senate. The House is comprised
of members elected from the individual states, with the
number of representatives allocated to each state based
upon the population of that state, with every state having at
least one. For instance, Wyoming has a population of only
481,000 people and therefore, has only 1 representative in
the House. Florida has a population of more than
15,000,000 and has 23 representatives in the House. Easy
enough, right?

Now, let's go to the Senate. The Senate is
comprised of 2 members from each state. "Wait one rott'n,
stink'n, minute here."

175

Oh, now you got it. Wyoming has 2 Senators from a state with only 481,000 people, while Florida also has two Senators, but with a population of more than 15,000,000.

Well, that just ain't fair, is it? Of course it's fair. Why? Because that's the deal that was cut between the states when we entered this agreement—America. That's the covenant, the promise, as it was presented to each state who chose to bind itself with the others in the form of our Constitution.

But what does that have to do with the Electoral College? I'm glad you asked. The Electoral College is comprised of a group of "electors" chosen by each state. The number of electors given to each state is equal to the number of Senators in the state (2) when added to the number of house representatives from that state.

Wyoming has 2 senators, plus 1 representative in the house. How many electors? 3.

Florida has 2 senators, plus 23 representatives in the house. That's right . . . 25 electors.

The process is not a complicated one, and it does insure that every state gets some voice in who the President may be. This election process is in our Constitution and it would require a Constitutional amendment to be ratified (approved) by three fourths of the states. Oh, there's that evil "state" thing again. The bottom line—don't hold your breath waiting for this one Myrtle, 'cause it ain't gonna happen.

X

The Final Count—
No Really, I Mean It This Time

Revenge of the He Coon?
I Don't Think So

Some people in our fair state are referring to the judiciousless order handed down by Little Chuckie Wells and the Florida Supremes as the "revenge of the He-Coon." I do not agree with that assessment. The assertion that the "Governor" was somewhat to the left of center may well be true. It is indeed a fact that he appointed "Little Chuckie Wells" and five of the other six members of the Florida Supremes, but it does not follow that the He Coon would relish or even condone the outrageous and self destructive order that came out of Tallahassee yesterday.

Yes, Chiles certainly had his battles with the Republican dominated Florida Legislature. Sometimes it even seemed like he enjoyed the fight, itself, more than winning. So what's the difference?

Chiles was a pragmatist and politically astute. He would have known that such a blatant political act by a supposed "a-political" judiciary would result in all members of the court being discharged when the next retention vote occurs for each of them. Jeb Bush will appoint their replacements and, within six years, the court will be comprised of seven Republican appointed justices. Chiles would recognize it as a terrible act of self-destruction and a set back for the only branch of state government still held by "de facto Democrats"; the one remaining check on Republican action.

I personally see it as a very sad turn of events. Not sad because these particular people will be "fired" from the Court, because each and every one of them should be fired.

But, rather, sad because no judiciary should ever be so partisan, whether appointed by Republicans or Democrats. I fear that this precedent has set a partisan tone that will be difficult to eradicate from the Florida judiciary.

Despite Chiles' fervor when engaging in the art of political haggling, I think the Governor would see this as a "judicial coup d'etat." Remember, the He Coon was a lawyer and he would recognize that the court ignored Florida law as well as the U.S. Constitution in rendering its decision. It is a dangerous arrogance.

Some Democrats will "poo-poo" my assessment of this.

I think that I know what the ol' He Coon would say about this "decision" of the Florida Supremes. He would call it like he saw it . . . "Heifer Dust!"

Have You Always Been an Idiot
or Is This a New Development?

Have you read the recent piece written by Richard Stengel for TIME? It's entitled "Good Clean Cheating and Dirty Pool." In it, Mr. Stengel attempts to draw a distinction between "good old honest cheating" like that done by Lyndon Johnson, who paid cash for his first Senate seat and the Chicago grave-robbing votes of Billy Bob's daddy, Richard Daley. "That" kind of cheating, Stengel contends is "good old-fashioned cheating," and is readily accepted by the American people. What Americans find unacceptable is hiring lawyers to go to court, according to Stengel, "to get people to abide by statutes, or to clear up murky ones, well, that's dirty pool." . . . or so he says.

Did TIME really pay you *American* money for writing this Mr. Stengel? I was just curious. I'm surprised that they would let a man that don't know no more than you do, work there in the first place. Mr. Stengel, you say that "there is a vague presumption among Americans that Gore is the down-and-dirty cheater and Bush is the honest cheater."

Let's look at your claims for a moment, Mr. Stengel. First, the cheating scoundrels Johnson and Daley (for the benefit of Kennedy/Johnson) were <u>all</u> Democrats. I see that fact seems to have slipped your mind when you wrote your article, Mr. Stengel. Secondly, the fact that no outrage was expressed by the public at large, merely indicates that Americans in general, were unaware of the activities of these crooks. We are offended by Billy Bob's attempts to "dig up" votes here in Florida.

The reason that Americans view the hoards of high-priced lawyers marching from court to court to court to court, as a dirty low down scum bucket trick to steal the election is because they have more than a "vague presumption" as you call it, that Bush has won the election.

Why? On election night, all of the networks called Gore the winner in Florida, although the polls were still open here in the Panhandle. What did Bush do? Concede? No. He publicly announced to the world that the networks were calling the show too soon, because the vote was not yet in from northwest Florida.

Ok, I'll admit that Bush's cousin at Fox News did announce that W. was the winner at 1:30 the next morning. But, what did Gore do? He called Bush and conceded the election, and get this; Albert calls himself the smart one.

The Florida vote was tallied and what-da-ya know—Bush won. It was recounted and, what-da-ya know, Bush won again. It has just been re-re-counted, and what-da-ya, what-da-ya, what-da-ya know—Bush again.

How did Gore's lawyers respond—"We will sue somebody, no matter how it comes out." Gee, Mr. Stengel, I can't imagine why the American people would find this unacceptable. Clarifying statues, or clearing "up murky ones," I don't think so. In Florida, Mr. Stengel, we know swamp scum when we see it.

You say that there is "a general sense that Bush has been 'out-lawyered', and that being 'out-lawyered' is down-right un-American." It *is* un-American Mr. Stengel. If you cared about the rule of law, then you would understand why that matters. For the record, Mr. Stengel, Bush wasn't really out-lawyered—they just went to a lynching with nothing but the U.S. Constitution. A mob, Mr. Stengel, even if they are wearing robes, generally doesn't care much about the law.

Even the craftiest lawyer should not be able to stand the law of our land on its head, shake the milk money from its pockets, and move on without a whimper from the people. What you are really saying is, "you let us [the Democrats] rob you before . . . Why are you complaining now?"

You also say, Mr. Stengel, that you are "growing a little weary of the Bush campaign's constant cry that Gore's lawyers changed the rules in the middle of the game." There's another *little problem* here Mr. Stengel, it's the United States Code; it's a set of books, they have laws written in them, Mr. Stengel, one of which, 3 U.S.C. § 5, prohibits the changing of the rules in the middle of the election. You see Mr. Stengel, when it's the seventh game of the World Series, bottom of the ninth and two outs and the batter at the plate swings—three strikes you're out—the game is over, that's just the rule. In America, we don't change the rules to give 'em four strikes or four outs. That would be "un-American," Mr. Stengel.

You ain't home-schooling your kids are you, Mr. Stengel? I hope not.

Finally, Mr. Stengel, you question why the electoral college itself is not viewed "as an example of legal pettifoggery." Legal pettifoggery indeed; you're so cleaver, Mr. Stengel. I ain't explaining that one again, please see my column—Hillary wants to scrap the College. But, to top it off, Mr. Stengel, you say the "dirty cheating" electoral college was, after all, created "by a handful of men in wigs in Philadelphia in 1787." About that "handful of men in wigs in Philadelphia in 1787," Mr. Stengel—you

ain't fit to shovel the s . . ., that is, to clean out the garage
where those men parked their horses.

If Albert Ain't Going . . .
I Ain't Either

November 25, 2000, Belgrade, Yugoslavia.

For all of us who heard the Presidential debate back on October 3rd, the question and answers now seem surreal.

Jim Lehrer: "Vice President Gore; if President Milosevic of Yugoslavia refuses to accept the election results and leave office, what action, if any should the United States take to get him out of there?"

Gore: "Well, Milosevic has lost the election. His opponent, Kostunica, has won the election. It's overwhelming, that Milosevic's government refuses to release the vote count. There's now a general strike going on. They're demonstrating. . . . The people of Serbia have acted very bravely in kicking this guy out of office. Now he is trying to tie up the votes."

Lehrer: "Governor Bush, one minute."

Bush: "It's time for the man to go."

Today, Slobodan Milosevic has reclaimed the position as leader of the Socialist Party. In his opening speech to the delegates to the party congress, Milosevic described those who sought his removal as, get this, "members of a vast right wing conspiracy out to destroy socialists."

Milosevic has reportedly contacted Gore's campaign anthropologist, Bill Daley, as well as top Gore lawyers, to assist him in the "undertaking." Like Slobadon said, "If Albert ain't going . . . I ain't either."

Just Who's Ox is Being "Gore-d" Here Anyway?

Can you believe all the commotion down in Palm Beach County? Law suits are flying through the Circuit Court Clerk's Office like fur in a cat fight. The Gore Campaign says they intend to join in the law suits which seek a new election there.

The Gore people ought to join in the law suits, they caused them to be filed in the first place. For the life of me, I just can't see what the problem is with that ballot. First, you find the name of the person you want to vote for— follow the arrow directly from the name to a punch mark, and then punch it out. What's the big deal here? I don't get it, and neither do my pals Eric & Meg @ Sunny 98.5. I do not know the identity of the author, but they sent me this:

"The Palm Beach Pokey"

You put your stylus in,
You put your stylus out,
You put your stylus in,
And you punch Buchanan out.
You do the Palm Beach Pokey
And you turn the count around,
That's what it's all about!

You put the Gore votes in,
You put the Bush votes out,
You put the Gore votes in,

Red Bugs, Moonshine and the Book of Leviticus

And you do another count.
You do the Palm Beach Pokey
And you turn the count around,
That's what it's all about!

You bring your lawyers in,
You drag the whole thing out,
You bring your lawyers in,
And you put it all in doubt.
You do the Palm Beach Pokey
And you turn the count around,
That's what it's all about!

You let your doctors spin,
You let the pundits spout,
You let your retirees sue,
And your people whine and pout.
You do the Palm Beach Pokey
And you turn the count around,
That's what it's all about!

You do the Palm Beach Pokey
You do the Palm Beach Pokey
You do the Palm Beach Pokey
That's what it's all about!

XI

Bill Daley—Won't You Please Go Home

Bill Daley—Won't You Please Go Home

On November 8, 2000, our lovely state was invaded by Gore Campaign operatives, William "Billy Bob" Daley and a hoard of scum sucking Yankee lawyers. What are they doing here, Mr. Gore? Oh, their just observing the votes. Yeah, right; and his daddy just liked to read the inscriptions on tomb stones.

Why do you think they are here?

    (a)   to encourage Secretary of State Harris to perform her duty and certify the election;

    (b)   to get a really nice tan;

    (c)   to ensure that the post office properly delivers each and every overseas military ballot; or

    (d)   to create problems in need of a law suit and then be suddenly available to fill the need.

How will Bill Daley's presence contribute to the "truthful" outcome of the Florida vote-tally?

    (a)   He'll ensure that every dead person has a voice in the election;

    (b)   He'll offer all election canvassing board members 8 million dollars and a Presidential pardon—should Gore just happen to win;

    (c)   He'll wander off into a swamp and get eaten by alligators, who upon digesting him will

Red Bugs, Moonshine and the Book of Leviticus

present the "results" as the truthful "outcome,"
or
(d)   He won't.

Come on Florida! Sing along . . .

> *Won't you go home, Bill Daley*
> *Won't you go home*
> *We moan the whole day long*
> *We'll drive you to the airport,*
> *We'll pay the flight*
> *You know you've done us wrong*
> *Bill Daley won't you PLEASE GO HOME?*

Military History

The telephone rang. "Mr. Revell, you don't know me, but may name is Dr. Alexander Hamilton Boatwright the 5th and I'm a professor of sociology at Kent State University," he began. "I'm conducting a study on the slanting of military historical facts by the victorious combatant," he continued.

"Dr. Boatwright, I think you've dialed the wrong number," I responded. "I don't know the first thing about the alteration of military facts for the sake of posterity. I do know that LBJ lied about the Tonkin Gulf incident, but that's already been corrected for our continued historical enjoyment."

"I would be more than willing to help you if I could, Dr. Boatwright, but I don't know anything about the subject, and besides I am really busy right now. I'm trying to figure out why one's wife would ask one, which pair of shoes looked better with a particular outfit and upon hearing one's opinion, one's wife would declare that one's wife's husband had no taste whatsoever. Why would one's wife ask anyone whom she believed to be devoid of 'taste' such a question in the first place. Secondly, what does that imply about such a 'tasteless' person's choice of a wife? What are your thoughts, Dr. Boatwright?"

"I'm afraid I can't help you with that one," Dr. Boatwright responded, "but, I don't think I would pose that second question to her."

Good advice, I thought.

"Mr. Revell, I'm not seeking your personal knowledge of altered military history. My specific focus is

193

on the American Civil War, and the quote, unquote facts as they have been taught in various regions of the country," he explained. This knowledge may provide me with information relating to the alteration of historical fact by the conqueror at the expense of the conquered."

"Which war are you focusing on, Dr. Boatwright?"

"The American Civil war."

"I don't think any war has ever been civil."

"I may agree with you on that point, Mr. Revell, but the war to which I am referring is The American Civil War."

"Are you talking about the War for Independence?"

"No! the war with General Lee."

"Would that be 'Light Horse' Harry or Robert Edward? I'm sorry Dr. Boatwright, but I am still confused as to exactly which war you are talking about. Why don't you give me the dates of the war to which you are referring, or at least some information by which I may identify the conflict."

"I'm referring to the war which began with the firing on Ft. Sumter, South Carolina, and ended with Lee's surrender to Grant at Appamadox Courthouse, Virginia. The Civil War."

"Who selected that name for that conflict, Dr. Boatwright?"

"Hell, I don't know."

"The war to which you refer, Dr. Boatwright, is the second American Revolution, that is, the war for Southern Independence."

The conversation fell silent for several seconds and then Dr. Boatwright responded, "It took me a while to catch on, didn't it, Mr. Revell?"

"I wouldn't feel too bad Dr. Boatwright. It didn't take you all that long to get it . . . at least not for a damn Yankee."

True Grit

I recently went into a pet shop just to browse. I had a few minutes to kill before an appointment. I suppose it's been more than a few years since I've been in a pet shop. When I was a child, I spent countless hours watching the birds, fish and fluffy little creatures for sale there.

The pet shop of my youth is no more. At least that's what the little girl with the earbob in her tongue said from behind the credit card machine. (I can even remember cash registers.) This particular store was more like a Wild Kingdom production than a pet shop. I kept looking for Jim Fowler to appear at any moment. I knew Marlin Perkins was safely hiding across the street or behind some snake-proof glass somewhere talking to somebody about insurance.

Anyway, pet shops used to sell puppies, kittens, hamsters, little white mice, parakeets, canaries, maybe a guinea pig or two and fish—mostly gold. Not anymore. They now sell "pets" that can injure or maim you. They even post signs warning of the danger.

"Iguana will bite!"

"Do not stick fingers into water—piranhas will bite."

"Do not stick fingers into cage—Codi Mundi will bite them off!"

And, "Please do not tap on glass" reads the sign on the snake aquariums.

"Don't you sell any Cocker Spaniels or parakeets or calico cats?" I asked.

"How old are you anyway?" Responded Earbob Tongue.

"Old enough not to spend no three hundred dollars on a snake," I replied. "I just killed a huge one in my garage yesterday, and if you charge by the pound—he'd have brought five hundred dollars or better."

"That's a horrible thing to do. Snakes are our best sellers and they are very intelligent and clean," she hissed.

"I'll say they're smart—it took me and my sledge hammer half an hour to track down that scaly forked-tongued demon and smash him into snake puree."

"I first saw him as he approached the main garage entry. I yelled at him. He ran (if a snake can run) behind some boxes and into the corner where he coiled into a circle."

I immediately thought of my last close encounter of the scaly kind. I was nine or ten at the time and my daddy and I were quail hunting. The dog flushed a covey and we dropped two of them—one about twenty yards away and the other a bit further fell into a patch of briars. I *let* the dog fetch the one in the briars. I put down my gun and began looking for the other one. Within seconds I heard that dreaded noise and I froze dead in my tracks. There, a foot and a half in front of me, was the mother of all snakes coiled in the hollow of an old tree stump and rattling its tail vigorously.

Daddy called out in a calm but commanding voice—STAND STILL. Being the obedient child that I was, I looked down at the snake and then bolted for the highway. I was half-way to Sopchoppy by the time Daddy caught up with me.

"Where are you going?" he asked.

"Ireland," I responded.

197

"Why Ireland?"

"I hear there ain't no snakes in Ireland."

"Get in the truck, son."

That was nearly thirty-five years ago and since then, I've given up running because it's an unhealthy activity. Running can cause you to have a heart attack or you could step on a rock and fall down and break your leg. I've now been to Ireland and learned that a terrorist bomb will kill you just as dead as a rattlesnake will. I could give the house to the snake, but I'd still have to pay the mortgage.

There was only one option—me or the snake. I climbed on top of a chair in case he chose to attack. I grabbed a post hole digger, leaning against the wall and raised it above the coiled snake looking carefully for his head. I couldn't identify head from tail. For the record, snakes as a part of their satanic nature are mind-readers. Just as I was about to slam him with the posthole digger, the snake took off to the other side of the garage as he regrouped to attack.

I had him on the run. I began tossing boxes from one end of the garage to the other as I searched for the menacing, slit-eyed, forked tongue devil. I found him stretched along the wall behind a sheet of plywood. He was a lot bigger than I had first thought. I reached for a sledge hammer and pounded the slimy monster into snake-burger.

"How could you do such a thing?" Earbob Tongue hissed as her pupils turned to slits and the earbob in her tongue began to rattle.

I bolted for the door. I was half way to Sopchoppy by the time I realized that I had left the truck parked in front of the snake shop. Maybe I will take up jogging.

Nullum Gratuitum Prandium

Don't you love it when Liberals accuse Conservatives of being heartless, mean, cruel, and uncharitable for refusing to give away *your* money to one of their pet projects. You know – those important matters of national concern, like paying an "artist" to photograph a man with a bullwhip in his rectum. Or maybe to photograph a "possum" (I know it's supposed to be spelled opossum – would you just leave it alone here please) that's been run over on the side of the road.

And if anyone has the good sense to point out the insanity of giving away the people's money for such a project – that person is ridiculed and called something like: "You heartless, insensitive, bigoted, Neanderthal."

Giving away someone else's money does not make you charitable. You want to be charitable? Give away your own money.

The people's money needs to be used for things like national defense, police and fire protection, education, roads, and yes – temporary economic relief for those who have fallen on hard times. That is, until they can get on their own feet again – with the emphasis on getting on their own feet. The only permanent relief programs should be for the elderly and those who are incapable of working – not for those who are capable, but won't.

I know, I know, I'm a "heartless, insensitive, bigoted, Neanderthal."

A dangerous concept has developed in our country. It is, that someone has a right to, or is "entitled" to welfare. The liberals have even changed the name.

They now call them – "entitlements." I guess it's a lost value, but I still believe it – You have no right to what doesn't belong to you.

About once a week, someone suggests that I run for a political office. My answer is always the same – I cain't stand politicians. Joe Scarborough apparently can't stand them either. He recently wrote a piece in which he described many of his fellow congressmen as being "full of themselves." A lot of them are full of something else too.

You can ask a politician a very simple question. Like – "Don't you think that homosexual men should have the right to be Boy Scout leaders and go out and sleep in the woods with little boys?" A politician will spend three hours discussing everything under the sun – that is, everything but your question. You eventually get tired and go away, and he doesn't have to answer your question. If someone asked me that same question, my answer would be short and to the point. I'd say, "Are you crazy? Perhaps you think that Bill Clinton ought to be in charge of organizing the Girl Scouts for their annual cookie campaign. Get away from me before somebody thinks that I know you."

If I ever did run for office, I would have a neck-tie specially made. It would have the Latin words printed on it, "Nullum Gratuitum Prandium." It means, "There ain't no such thing as a free lunch."

XII

What's Next?
How Would I Know, Do I
Look Like Jeane Dixon?

What's Next?
How Would I Know, Do I
Look Like Jeane Dixon?

November 27, 2000, Santa Rosa Beach.

Will this thing ever end?   Last night, Florida Secretary of State Katherine Harris, certified the election for W. Albert says that he has just begun to fight, and his lawyers will start suing counties right and left today.

The Right Wrong Rev. Al Sharpton is in Dade County planning another riot, since Jesse and his rioteers failed to stir up much of a commotion in Palm Beach County two weeks ago.

What are all of these lawyers and marchers going to accomplish? Nothing. Absolutely nothing.

One of Gore's lawyers has tipped his hand. "The problem here," he says, "is that the bickering is 'too clean.' There's no fraud. If only there was some fraud."

"I once got an election overturned," he claims, "by showing that supposed absentee ballots were not actually cast by the voters. That's what we need here."

I wouldn't worry too much, Mr. Gore lawyer. For the right amount of money, I'm sure that Bill Daley can dig up some people who will say just that or whatever else you want them to say.

I know that I am sticking my neck out with this prediction, but as of this day, November 27, here's how I think it will play out.

W. will act like the President-elect. He will have his lawyers quietly defend all actions pursued by the "Sore-Loserman" campaign.

The GOP will portray Albert, perhaps rightly so, as a raving madman in urgent need of some ridelin.

Gore will hide behind a big tree and watch as his pundits and lawyers deliver the "raving madman" threats to get really mean about this if W. doesn't let him live in the Whitehouse.

The U.S. Supreme Court will decide that Little Chuckie Wells and the Florida Supremes are in serious need of a lesson on Constitutional Government. They will supply the lesson.

The news media won't have the slightest idea what Justice Renquist and the sho' nuff Supremes write in their decision, so they'll just say: U.S. Supreme Court finds for Bush. The American people will think; that's the ball game; and so it will be.

A handful of radical Congressional Democrats from safe districts, like loud-mouth, Robert Wexler, will file a formal objection to Congressional acceptance of the Florida electoral vote.

Ted Kennedy, or some other half-crocked nit-wit, will do the same on the Senate side.

Here we go again. But wait, house districts are being redrawn following the 2000 census. House Democrats don't know what their district will look like when next they beg for votes. Gore's support will simply blow away in the breeze.

Albert will lay on the floor, pouting, kicking and screaming. He may even refuse to surrender the Vice President's mansion to Cheney. If that were to happen, the U.S. Marshals (where's John Wayne when you need him?)

would conduct the eviction. All the while Albert will be screaming . . . "But I am the President, really. Why don't you believe me?"

Constitutional Government 101

December 4, 2000, Washington D.C.

I hate to say "I told you so," but, "I told you so." Well, I don't really hate it that much. Ok, the truth is, I'm doing back flips about it. The U.S. Supremes backhanded Little Chuckie Wells and the Florida Supremes today. The press is running to and fro looking for someone to explain what the Sho' 'Nuff Supremes intended by the text of its decision. One reporter simply said, "U.S. Supreme Court reverses Florida Supreme Court ruling." Another said, "Confused U.S. Supreme Court sends case back to Florida Supreme Court." Others just threw up their hands and asked Democrats in Congress, "Did the fat lady just sing a solo to Albert?"

First of all, let me explain that the U.S. Supreme Court is not the least bit confused about this case. The justices of this court as well as the law clerks that assist them are some of the brightest legal minds in the country.

In returning the case to the Florida Supremes, the "Sho' 'Nuffs" ask several rhetorical questions accompanied by comments. It's intellectual legal jousting, that's all. Poking fun, if you will. Let me translate:

SHO' 'NUFFS: The [Florida Supreme] Court then stated: "Because of our reluctance to rewrite the Florida Election Code, we conclude that we must invoke the equitable powers of this Court to fashion a remedy . . ." The Court thus imposed a deadline for return of the ballot counts . . . effectively extend[ing] the [deadline] by 12 days.

TRANSLATION: You obviously were not too reluctant to rewrite the election code; you did it. You probably don't know that the legislature is supposed to write laws and you are supposed to interpret them.

SHO' 'NUFFS: As a general rule, this Court defers to a state court's interpretation of a state statute. But in the case of a law enacted by a state legislature applicable not only to elections to state offices, but also to the selection of Presidential electors, the legislature is not acting solely under the authority given it by the people of the State, but by virtue of a direct grant of authority made under Art. II, sec. 1, cl. 2, of the United States Constitution. That provision reads:

> "Each State shall appoint, in such Manner as the Legislature thereof may direct, a Number of Electors, equal to the whole Number of Senators and Representatives to which the State may be entitled in the Congress . . ."

TRANSLATION: You did know there was a U.S. Constitution didn't you? In case you don't have a copy, let us tell you what the pertinent article says.

SHO' 'NUFFS: Art. II, sec. 1, cl. 2 [the U.S. Constitution] does not read that the people or the citizens shall appoint, but that 'each State shall'; and if the words 'in such manner as the legislature thereof may direct,' had been omitted, it would seem that the legislative power of

207

appointment could not have been successfully questioned in the absence of any provision in the state constitution in that regard. Hence the insertion of those words, while operating as a limitation upon the State in respect of any attempt to circumscribe the legislative power, cannot be held to operate as a limitation on that power itself.

TRANSLATION: Do you see how carefully we analyze the law? That's what you are supposed to be doing, you morons. Oh yeah; one more thing, you cain't twist the Florida Constitution to override the U.S. Constitution—that dog won't hunt.

SHO' 'NUFFS: After reviewing the opinion of the Florida Supreme Court, we find 'that there is considerable uncertainty as to the precise grounds for the decision.' This is sufficient reason for us to decline at this time to review the federal question asserted to be present.

TRANSLATION: After reading your decision 406 times, we still cain't figure out what law you relied upon to come up with that piece of . . . well . . . what you wrote. It just don't make no sense. We've seen more well reasoned, legally sound decisions come out of the 4th grade moot court competition in Jackson, Mississippi.

SHO' 'NUFFS: "It is fundamental that state courts be left free and unfettered by us in interpreting their state constitutions. But it is equally important that ambiguous or obscure adjudications by state courts do not stand as barriers to a determination by this court of the validity under the federal constitution of state action. Intelligent exercise of our appellate powers compels us to ask for the elimination of the obscurities and ambiguities from the opinions in such cases."

TRANSLATION: We really don't want to stick our nose in Florida's 'bidness', but when you thought you could completely ignore the law and the Constitution and pick the President yourself, you thought wrong.

And about that decision you people wrote . . . Y'all weren't smoking crack when you wrote that thing, were you? Maybe you should look into doing something else. We understand that there is a big need for zoo-keepers in Florida.

SHO' 'NUFFS: The judgment of the Supreme Court of Florida is therefore vacated.

TRANSLATION: You people probably need a vacation.

As if the decision of the U.S. Supreme Court wasn't enough, Leon County Circuit Judge Sandy Sauls issued his ruling today. In short, the decision reads:

"Go home Albert and take Bill Daley and David Boies with ya'."

People Who Talk To God

Some people have complained that this piece reflects an anti-Catholic bias. It does not. For the record – does anyone know of another human being who has demonstrated the love of Christ more vividly than the late Mother Teresa or Pope John Paul II? I don't.

There once was a boy named Randall. He was born in a small town in France. Randall and his family were winemakers. Randall and some of his kin-folk believed that they could pray directly to God. Most of the people in France thought that Randall should pray to a "saint" or else ask a priest to talk to God for them.

The church folks said that Randall and his family were in disobedience to the church. Randall said he was being obedient to God, and nothing else mattered. Before long, most folks got fed up with Randall and his kind talking straight to God and they complained to the French government. The government told Randall to "stop that praying right now," but he wouldn't stop talking to God. Randall and his kin folks and all others in France like them were called Huguenots. In some other places they were just called Protestants. One weekend when the Huguenots came to Paris to pray, the government ordered the army to put an end to the Huguenots' rebellious behavior once and for all. Ten thousand French Protestants were slaughtered in the streets in a single day just outside Paris. Randall and all his family were shocked and took up their weapons hoping that the slaughter would not continue. The

Huguenots were outnumbered about a half million to one. As Randall marched off to battle, he asked God to give him victory that he and his descendants could live in their own land in peace. He fought at the battle of La Rochelle. The Huguenots lost. Randall's soul was crushed. Had God rejected his petition?

Randall told his parents that maybe they should consider moving on to another place. "But we are French," his mother replied, "where could we go?" Randall's father decided that they would go to England where the country was full of Protestants and they would be accepted and could finally live in peace. They settled in the town of Bristol. Randall commented: "Certainement, ces personnes parlent d'une meniere e'trange, n'est-ce-pas, papa." Which translated into North Floridian means: "These people sho' do talk funny, don't they daddy?"

Randall's daddy replied, "Son, I told you they spoke a different language here." You'll learn it—we all will."

Randall and his family soon found that England was not the Protestant paradise for which they were searching. England was itself Protestant, but their King—Charles I, was not and within a couple of years, King Charles determined that he needed to wage war against the Scots, an action which would ultimately bring Britain into full civil war, Randall wanted no part of it. He said, "I've had enough of this—I'm going to America." And he did.

Randall was only twenty-something when he stepped onto the eastern Virginia /Maryland shore. He was enthusiastic about his new home and worked hard to acquire land there. He fell head over heals in love and married a beautiful young woman named Katherine Scarborough. Lord Calvert took notice of Randall and appointed him one of the original commissioners to oversee land grants in Somerset County. Randall became a member of the Virginia House of Burgesses representing Northampton County. Years later, when Lord Calvert desired to build a courthouse for Somerset county, he came to Randall. Randall was pleased to give 20 of his prime acres along the bank of the Manokin river for the project. Randall had four sons and four daughters and enough grandchildren to start his own baseball league. God had indeed heard Randall and had answered his prayer to give him and his descendants victory and peace in their own land.

It was certainly not what Randall had expected, but it was better than he could have ever dreamed.

Randall Revell died on May 27, 1685. He was 77 years old.

My son, I know that a lot of other blood also flows through your veins, but I thought you might like to know just how you came about that name.

XIII

Epilogue

Epilogue—

W's Victory Speech, Finally

Last night, Vice President Albert conceded the presidential election on nationwide radio and television with a promise not to "un-concede" this time. Within minutes, President-elect, W., took to the airwaves. Here is what he said:

"My fellow Americans, I appreciate so very much the opportunity to speak with you tonight. Mr. Speaker, Lt. Governor, distinguished guests, our country has been through a long and trying period, with the outcome of the presidential election not finalized for longer than any of us could ever imagine. Vice President Gore and I put our hearts and hopes into our campaigns; we both gave it our all. We shared similar emotions. So I understand how difficult this moment must be for Vice President Gore and his family. He has a distinguished record of service to our country as a congressman, a senator and as Vice President.

This evening I received a gracious call from the Vice President. We agreed to meet early next week in Washington and we agreed to do our best to heal our country after this hard-fought contest.

Tonight, I want to thank all the thousands of volunteers and campaign workers who worked so hard on my behalf. I also salute the Vice President and his supporters for waging a spirited campaign, and I thank him for a call that I know was difficult to make. Laura and I wish the Vice President and Sen. Lieberman and their families the very best.

I have a lot to be thankful for tonight. I am thankful for America and thankful that we are able to resolve our electoral differences in a peaceful way. I am thankful to the American people for the great privilege of being able to serve as your next president. I thank my wife and our daughters for their love. Laura's active involvement as first lady has made Texas a better place, and she will be a wonderful first lady for America.

I am proud to have Dick Cheney by my side, and America will be proud to have him as our next Vice President.

Tonight, I choose to speak from the chamber of the Texas House of Representatives, because it has been home to bipartisan cooperation. Here, in a place where Democrats have the majority, Republicans and Democrats have worked together to do what is right for the people we represent. We've had spirited disagreements, and in the end, we found constructive consensus. It is an experience I will always carry with me, and an example I will always follow.

I thank my friend, House Speaker Pete Laney, a Democrat, who introduced me today. And I want to thank the legislators of both political parties with whom I worked.

Across the hall in our Texas Capitol is the State Senate, and I cannot help but think of our mutual friend, the former Democrat Lieutenant Governor Bob Bullock. His love for Texas and his ability to work in a bipartisan way continue to be a model for all of us. The spirit of cooperation I have seen in this hall is what is needed in Washington, D.C. It is the challenge of our moment.

Epilogue

After a difficult election, we must put politics behind us and work together to make the promise of America available to every one of our citizens. I am optimistic that we can change the tone in Washington, D.C. I believe things happened for a reason, and I hope the long wait of the last five weeks will heighten a desire to move beyond the bitterness and partisanship of the recent past.

Our nation must rise above a house divided. Americans share hopes and goals and values far more important than any political disagreement.

Republicans want the best for our nation. And so do Democrats. Our votes may differ, but not our hopes.

I know America wants reconciliation and unity. I know Americans want progress. And we must seize this moment and deliver. Together, guided by a spirit of common sense, common courtesy and common goals, we can unite and inspire the American citizens.

Together, we will work to make all our public schools excellent, teaching every student of every background and every accent, so that no child is left behind.

Together, we will save Social Security and renew its promise of a secure retirement for generations to come.

Together we will strengthen Medicare and offer prescription drug coverage to all of our seniors.

Together, we will give Americans the broad, fair and fiscally responsible tax relief they deserve.

Together, we will have a bipartisan foreign policy true to our values and true to our friends. And we will have a military equal to every challenge, and superior to every adversary.

Together, we will address some of society's deepest problems one person at a time, but encouraging and

217

empowering the good hearts and good works of the American people. This is the essence of compassionate conservatism, and it will be a foundation of my administration.

These priorities are not merely Republican concerns or Democratic concerns, these are American responsibilities.

During the fall campaign, we differed about details of these proposals—but there was remarkable consensus about the important issues before us: excellent schools, retirement and health security, tax relief, a strong military and a more civil society.

We have discussed our difference; now it is time to find common ground and build consensus to make America a beacon of opportunity in the 21st century.

I am optimistic this can happen. Our future demands it, and our history proves it. Two hundred years ago, in the election of 1800, America faced another close presidential election. A tie in the Electoral College put the outcome into the hands of Congress.

After six days of voting, and 36 ballots, the House of Representatives elected Thomas Jefferson the third president of the United States. That election brought the first transfer of power from one party to another in our new democracy.

Shortly after the election, Jefferson, in a letter titled "Reconciliation and Reform," wrote this: "the steady character of our countrymen is a rock to which we may safely moor . . . . Unequivocal in principle, reasonable in manner, we shall be able to hope to do a great deal of good to the cause of freedom and harmony."

Two hundred years have only strengthened the steady character of America. And so, as we begin the work of healing our nation, tonight I call upon that character: respect for each other, respect for our difference, generosity of spirit, and a willingness to work hard and work together to solve any problem.

I have something else to ask you—to ask every American. I ask for you to pray for this great nation. I ask your prayers for leaders from both parties. I thank you for your prayers for me and my family, and I ask you to pray for Vice President Gore and his family. I have faith that with God's help, we as a nation will move forward together, as one nation, indivisible. And together we will create an America that is open, so every citizen has access to the American dream. An America that is educated, so every child has the keys to realize that dream. And an America that is united in our diversity and our shared American values that are larger than race or party.

I was not elected to serve one party, but to serve one nation. The president of the United States is the president of every single American of every race and every background. Whether you voted for me or not, I will do my best to serve your interest, and I will work to earn your respect.

I will be guided by President Jefferson's sense of purpose—to stand for principle, to be reasonable in manner, and, above all, to do great good for the cause of freedom and harmony. The presidency is more than a honor, more than an office. It is a charge to keep, and I will give it my all.

Thank you very much, and God bless America."

That was last night—

Today , demonstrations were held here in Florida, in which racist demagogues pitched their filth to seemingly

219

hungry crowds. They vowed to turn out in mass "next time" and "get" Jeb Bush, the president elect's brother. It was more like an old rally of the Klan, than a political function. Jesse Jackson accused Jeb of "Nazi tactics" and of targeting Holocaust victims.

This is the same Jesse Jackson who, while running for President referred to New York City as "Hymietown." Yes indeed Jesse, we know of your sincere deep and longstanding concern for the Jewish people. And this is the same Jeb Bush who has been married to a woman of color for more than 25 years. It seems a favorite tactic of the left today, to refer to Republicans as "Nazis." It strikes me that these people fail to recognize the import of the term. As Jonah Goldberg wrote in a brilliant piece in National Review:

"Calling someone a Nazi is as bad as calling them a 'nigger' or a 'kike' or anything else you can think of. It's not cute. It's not funny. And it certainly is not clever. If you're too stupid to understand that a philosophy that favors a federally structured republic, with numerous restraints on the scope and power of government to interfere with individual rights or the free market, is a lot different from an ethnic-nationalist, atheistic, and socialist program of genocide and international aggression, you should use this rule of thumb: If someone isn't advocating the murder of millions of people in gas chambers and a global Reich for the White Man you shouldn't assume he's a Nazi and you should know it's pretty damn evil to call him one. . . ."

It's no wonder that many black people continue to feel alienated from American society; that seems to be all that their self appointed leaders ever talk about. I ask you—how do issues important to black people differ from the ones important to white people?

You cain't enter the Promised Land without first leaving the slavery of Egypt. And one more point—the Promised Land is not a place where Pharaoh provides you with a subsistence living. That's still slavery. It's a lot easier to give mindless speeches about hatred than to enter the debate seeking honest solutions. Focusing on victimization and then "feeling your pain" seems to be a surefire way of getting elected. It's so sad.

It is particularly sad when you consider that finally the mainstream of the American people stand with open arms, anxious and ready to welcome people of every color into the fold. As a child, I never really thought that I would see the dawn of that day, but it has dawned. Thank God. The question now is; will black leaders put the interest of their constituents first and encourage the integration? Or will they put their own interests first, as leaders of a segregated people?

Can't we just be Americans? Please?